Also by William Garrett:

*Bad Karma: Thinking Twice about the Social
Consequences of Reincarnation Theory* (2005)

Marie Stopes: Feminist, Eroticist, Eugenicist

Essential Writings

Edited and Introduced by
William Garrett

Kenon Books®
San Francisco

To Judy Marie Wilson— personal coach, executive consultant, spiritual advisor, confidant, relentless sergeant-major, dog wrangler, chef, resident jester. And a soul-mate that I had no sensible reason to expect in my life.

CONTENTS

INTRODUCTION: William Garrett, Ph.D.

MARIE STOPES: ESSENTIAL WRITINGS

ACKNOWLEGEMENTS

I am fortunate to have relentlessly inquisitive and demanding students at John F. Kennedy University— they prompt me both to clarity and to audacity, and I here gratefully acknowledge their influence. In addition, I express my thanks to members of the John F. Kennedy University library staff who provided expert assistance in gathering the writings of Marie Stopes presented in this volume: Joan Bewley, Thereza Cheng, and Steven Moody. They found manuscripts that were known to be unfindable, and they made it look easy. Finally, I appreciate having benefitted from the generosity and superb editorial skills of Amy Altschul, whose hawkeye assessments and patient explanations have made the text of my introductory essay far more lucid than it would otherwise have been.

William Garrett
Alameda, California, 2007

Introduction
William Garrett, PhD

Marie Stopes and the Daughter of Time

> For, truth is rightly named the daughter of time,
> not of authority. It is not wonderful, therefore, if
> the bonds of antiquity, authority, and unanimity,
> have so enchained the power of man, that he is
> unable (as if bewitched) to become familiar with
> things themselves.
>
> Francis Bacon, *Novum Organum 84*

1

Bacon's elegant metaphor of truth as the daughter of
time is designed to remind us of something obvious to
anyone with even a cursory acquaintance with history: the
truth by which we live is a *human* truth, and as such is
subject to revision, even reversal, over time. Truth—
whether about religion, about nature, about society, about
human nature— is time's daughter in that all her declarations
are *provisional;* her claims are without exception situated in

and conditioned by time, by the values and biases of a certain historical period.

But you needn't read history. If you live long enough, even for a few decades, you only need to keep your eyes and your mind open to verify Bacon's claim. The consensus about what is righteous and what is not, the considered opinion of reputable experts— these, the experience of a few decades shows us, are *fluid* verities. And this fluidity is handsomely evident in the varieties of wickedness ascribed to Marie Stopes.

In her heyday, during the second and third decades of the 20th century, Marie Stopes was vilified for her advocacy of birth-control. But she was even more vilified for her strident and (to decent people of the time) excruciatingly explicit assertions that women are possessed of an equally vigorous sexual appetite as are men. For such assertions, Stopes was seen by many of her contemporaries as sexually deranged and as little more than a smut peddler.

In our day, here at the beginning of the 21st century, Marie Stopes is again vilified— but for very different reasons. By now, her views on the sexuality of women are taken as entirely unremarkable. But when the name Marie Stopes is mentioned these days, the topic is usually not sexuality. Today she is remembered, if at all, not as a sexual revolutionary, but as standing among the dark cabal of those intellectuals who advocated *eugenics.* Eugenics: the theory that, it is popularly assumed, served as the centerpiece of National Socialist (i.e., Nazi) ideology. Indeed, the very word eugenics is for many in the 21st century a byword for racism and genocide.

In her day, Stopes' advocacy of birth-control and her assertion of the realities of female sexuality were condemned by the prevailing authorities as appallingly wicked; in our day the prevailing authorities see such recommendations as common sense. In her day, Stopes' advocacy of eugenics was taken by the prevailing authorities to be common sense; in our day the prevailing authorities see such recommendations as appallingly wicked. *Truth is rightly named the daughter of time, not of authority.*

What is presented in this volume is a selection of texts that represents the essential thinking and character of Marie Stopes. Care was taken to include selections that are especially relevant to the project of rethinking the world of the 21st century. Some of what is included has previously been most difficult to access— specifically, her 1920 pamphlet *A New Gospel for All the People* and her 1919 newspaper article "How Mrs. Jones Does Her Worst," as well as selections from her 1928 book, *Enduring Passion.*

Throughout this Introduction, citations from texts included in the Sources will reference title and page number in this volume— for example, *Radiant Motherhood,* p. 48. References to other works cited will be found in endnotes following the Introduction.

2

Biographical Sketch

Marie Carmichael Stopes was born in Edinburgh, Scotland, on October 15, 1880. Her father, Henry Stopes, was trained as an engineer, and worked designing breweries. But his real enthusiasm was for archaeology. Marie would visit him on various of his excavations, and her relationship to him was close until his death in 1902.

Marie Stopes' mother, Charlotte Carmichael, earned a University certificate— she was awarded a *certificate* rather than a degree, despite the fact that she'd done the same work as the male students, because at this time in Great Britain women were not awarded *degrees*. Charlotte seethed about this injustice throughout her life; she became an ardent feminist and suffragette; she was a member of the Rational Dress Society (a protest movement against the tortuously constrictive dress code for "ladies" in the Victorian era); she was also a respected Shakespeare scholar.

A strong disposition to feminism came to Marie, as it were, through her mother's milk. But throughout her long life, until she died in 1929 at the age of eighty-eight, Charlotte Stopes was a psychological burden to her illustrious daughter— jealous of Marie's fame, greedy for her money, endlessly critical of every aspect of her personality.

In her youth, Marie was relatively indifferent to study. But when she entered higher education, she came into her element. She earned a B.Sc. in science (honors in Botany and Geology) at University College, London, in 1902. She went to the Botanical Institute of the University of Munich— where she was the only woman graduate student— and in 1904 she earned a PhD. in paleobotany (ancient botany). Marie Stopes became recognized as one of the world's foremost authorities in coal. The next year, 1905, she earned an even more prestigious scientific degree, a D.Sc., from the University of London. She was the youngest D.Sc. in Great Britain.

While studying for her PhD. in Munich, she met another non-German— a Japanese scientist named Kenjiro Fujii. There was attraction between the two, and despite the fact the Fujii already had a wife and child, Stopes developed marriage plans with him. To be close to him, she arranged to spend some two years in Japan— from 1907 to 1909. Although romantic relationships between a European and an Asian are entirely unremarkable in the 21st century, this was emphatically not the case in 1907. Then, such a relationship was grudgingly accepted between a European man and an

Asian woman— recall Puccini's *Madama Butterfly.*
Grudgingly accepted, but never really respected. On the
other hand, love between a European *woman* and an Asian
man was taken to be, at least by Europeans, shocking and
depraved.

Social conventions and shocked proprieties aside, the
love between Drs. Stopes and Fujii did not work out. Given
the intensity and idiosyncrasies of Marie's character, it was
no doubt sensible that Fujii extricated himself from the
relationship. Marie returned to Scotland in 1909.

It was she who had left Fujii, but Marie was both
heartbroken and humiliated by the experience. Her strategy
for dealing with her pain was in questionable taste: she
published selections from her correspondence with Fujii in
the form of a novel, written under the pseudonym of G. N.
Mortlake. The purported fiction, titled *Love Letters of a
Japanese,* was published in 1911. In the story, as she tells it,
Marie is represented as Mertyl Meredith and Fujii as Kenrio
Watanabe. It is a story of emotional betrayal in which the
hopes and agonies of her unconsummated relationship with
Fujii are related. It is telling, perhaps, that the pseudonym
under which Stopes wrote the account, Mortlake, means
literally "lake of death." Another literary lament is found in
her 1908 poem, "The Idealist's Love," written while she was
in Tokyo:

> My lover hurt me, but I would not moan:
> For love was mine, and I was his alone.
> What though my lover as a mortal man
> Did break his truth — no mortal ever can
> Do all he would. I had no wish to blame
> And kissed his lying lips next day the same.[1]

Later in her life, when she was a recognized authority on
marriage and sexuality, Dr. Marie Stopes typically advised
those who consulted her *against* inter-racial marriage— very

likely an echo of the stinging disappointment she experienced through the first great love in her life.

Her second venture into love was even less fortunate. In 1911 Marie was doing research in Canada, where she met and fell in love with a geneticist named Reginald Ruggles Gates. For a time, all was well. But that, as Marie later reported, was because both she and her husband were desperately ignorant of the facts of human sexuality. Gates, who seems to have been a decent enough young man, was by disposition conventional and, far worse for Marie, sexually impotent. Married to Gates for five years, Marie Stopes was still a virgin when their divorce was finalized, a condition certified by her physician, Dr. E. Taylor— "I have today examined Dr Marie Stopes: in my opinion there is evidence from the condition of the hymen that there has not been penetration by a normal male organ."[2]

With a candor that served to establish her credibility among her many adoring readers (and which was seen as grotesque and tasteless by her adversaries), Stopes refers to her painful first marriage in the Preface to her bestselling book, *Married Love:*

> In my own marriage I paid such a terrible price for sex-ignorance that I feel that knowledge gained at such a cost should be placed at the service of humanity. In this little book average, healthy, mating creatures will find the key to the happiness which should be the portion of each. *Married Love,* p. 3

The marriage between Marie Stopes and Gates ended in 1916, not in divorce but in annulment— because of non-consummation. In 1918, at the age of thirty-seven and still a virgin, she married for a second time. Her second husband, Humphrey Verdon Roe, was a man of some wealth, and with him Stopes at last came to experience the sexuality that had, perhaps understandably, become so central to her psychological life.

On July 17, 1919, Marie's first child, a boy, arrived—alas, stillborn. A second male child, this time healthy, was born by Caesarean section on March 27, 1924. Harry Verdon Stopes-Roe was a healthy baby, but his birth was hard on Marie and she was informed that she should have no more children. Convinced that her son needed a companion and sibling, Marie advertised for one. She specified the following terms "A client in a very good position is desirous of adopting (complete adoption) a little boy between the ages of 20 months and 2¼ years. . . The child must be absolutely healthy, intelligent and not circumcised."[3] Cherished and over-cherished, young Harry found his life micro-managed by his indefatigable mother. Yet over the years he developed the grit needed to stand up to the mighty psychological force of Marie Stopes— a grit he doubtlessly inherited from her. He fell in love with and decided to marry a woman that his formidable mother thought beneath him. Harry's beloved, Mary Wallis, was deemed inappropriate by Marie because she wore glasses. Harry stood firm and the two married (and, it should be noted, the two lived happily). But Mother was not a good sport in the face of her son's self-assertion: although they remained on polite terms, she disinherited him.

Conflict and controversy were essential to Marie's life and character. Her first book, *Married Love,* was what we today would call a blockbuster. The book was given equal measures of lavish praise and savage vilification. There were, as we'll see in what follows, some good reasons for both extreme responses. A dedicated feminist, Stopes saw feminism as rooted in a radically different relation of women to sexuality. At issue for her was not just women's control of reproduction— birth control— but also a more realistic understanding of female sexuality. Her views on both topics drew the hostile attentions of conservative forces in British society.

Antagonism toward Marie Stopes grew steadily since the publication of *Married Love* in 1918. A typical expression of this was published in 1919 by the periodical *New Witness*. In its edition of September 12, 1919, Stopes' ideas were attacked through an assault on her own character and that of one of her prominent supporters, Arnold Bennett, who had written an Introduction to *Wise Parenthood:*

> After much consideration we have decided that a thundering attack would please this most unpleasant woman almost as well as ardent support . . . The peculiar horror of her book is that it is couched in pseudo-scientific terms, and is addressed to the married woman . . . Mr Arnold Bennett bears an honorable name: he can hope to bear it no longer if he does not at once dissociate himself from Dr Marie Stopes and her rubber goods. The introduction he has written to her filthy book is a disgrace to him and to his (and our) profession.[4]

The temper of this invective intensified to the point at which Marie could no longer ignore it. A physician and a recent convert to Roman Catholicism, Dr. Halliday G. Sutherland, with broad Catholic encouragement, published a polemic against birth control that singled out Dr. Marie Stopes for particular opprobrium. Published in March of 1922, *Birth Control: a Statement of Christian Doctrine against the Neo-Malthusians,* Sutherland made the following claim in a section titled "Specially Hurtful to the Poor: Exposing the Poor to Experiment"—

> . . . the ordinary decent instincts of the poor are against these [birth control] practices, and indeed they have used them less than any other class. But, owing to their poverty, lack of learning, and helplessness, the poor are the natural victims of those who seek to make experiments on their fellows. In the midst of a London slum a woman, who is a doctor of German philosophy (Munich), has opened a Birth Control Clinic, where working women are instructed in a method of

contraception described by Professor McIlroy as "the most harmful method of which I have had experience." When we remember that millions are being spent by the Ministry of Health and by Local Authorities . . . all for the single purpose of bringing healthy children into our midst, it is truly amazing that this monstrous campaign of birth control should be tolerated by the Home Secretary. Charles Bradlaugh was condemned to jail for a less serious crime.[5]

It was just this passage that, for Marie, went over the line. She was portrayed as "a doctor of German philosophy (Munich)." Yes, Stopes had earned a PhD at the University of Munich, and a PhD is a "doctor of philosophy" degree. But as we've seen, her degree was a *science* degree, a PhD in *paleobotany.* Sutherland's words were calculated to misrepresent Stopes, to place her among other exponents of "German philosophy" that were so notorious to the British public at the time— names like Heinrich von Treitschke and Friedrich Nietzsche, both of whom had been effectively scripted in British anti-German propaganda during the recent Great War as militarists and sadists in the mold of Attila the Hun.

Worse, Sutherland accused her of preying upon the very people she intended to help. Dr. Marie Stopes, the passage implied, was using the defenseless poor as experimental animals in social programs that were more than misdirected— they were irresponsible to the point of being criminal, and the incarceration of Dr. Stopes would constitute a satisfactory remedy. To speak for a moment from a 21st century perspective, Marie Stopes and her work with the poor were being cast as a kind of prequel to Dr. Josef Mengele and his ghastly and criminal experiments on the inmates at the Auschwitz concentration camp.

Stopes' indignation at Sutherland's characterization of her work brought her to embark on the most disruptive and distracting episode in her professional life. What was about to unfold was more than a confrontation between Dr. Marie Stopes and Dr. Halliday G. Sutherland. Conservative Christians, and especially the Roman Catholic Church, had nursed grudges against Stopes since her publication of *Married Love* in 1918, and her vigorous advocacy of birth control since then. And the Catholic Church in particular began to funnel monetary resources into Sutherlands's camp. When the case of Stopes v. Sutherland was opened on February 21, 1923, the issues ran far deeper and far more hotly than in more ordinary academic spats.

The jury's verdict was presented in a week— a confusing verdict in which Sutherland's statements were judged to be both defamatory and *true*. The judge, hostile to Stopes and the cause of birth control, found in favor of Sutherland. Stopes appealed on July 20, and had the decision reversed in her favor. Dr. Sutherland then appealed to the House of Lords, and on November 21, 1924 the verdict was again reversed— this time in Sutherland's favor. No further appeal was allowed. The case was finished, and Marie Stopes had lost. She was embittered, and for the rest of her life saw herself at war with the Catholic Church. While the Church saw its victory of a triumph of morality, Stopes saw it as a triumph of ignorance. And she was not alone in this assessment. As George Bernard Shaw wrote her a week after the final verdict:

> My dear Marie Stopes—
> The decision is scandalous; but I am not too surprised at it: the opposition can always fall back on simple taboo. The subject is obscene: no lady would dream of alluding to it in a mixed society: reproduction is a shocking subject and there's an end of it. You may get a temporary success by luring the enemy out of that last ditch where there is no defence but argument; but the only result is to drive them back into the ditch; and then you are done; the taboo is impregnable...[6]

Her battles with the Catholic Church and Dr. Sutherland were not over, however. In 1928 a Catholic woman, claiming to be instructed to do so by God, set fire to a mobile birth-control clinic used by Stopes. In 1929 Stopes published an angry statement that the Catholics were resorting to their old medieval practice of burning rather than debating their adversaries. Sutherland promptly sued for libel, but this time lost his case. Marie won, but the strain of the hostilities was beginning to tell on her. Her biographer Ruth Hall notes unhappy psychological effects that had manifested: "By 1928, her personality had changed— or, rather, rigidified into a pattern that had always been incipient."[7]

Marie Stopes had never been comfortable with criticism, but by the 1930s her defensiveness had begun to alienate her from valuable allies— people such as Bertrand Russell and H. G. Wells. A physician friend who'd known her over the course of a decade visited her in 1928 and described her as "suffering from two very grave pathological diseases— can you guess what they were? Yes, paranoia and megalomania."[8]

For the remainder of her life Stopes continued to publish, but her most important books and articles were behind her. Her marriage to Humphrey Verdon Roe was beginning to pale— mostly because Humphrey lacked the force of personality necessary to hold his own with the fiery character of Marie. There was no divorce, but Humphrey gave Marie written consent to take on lovers in July of 1938. And, no doubt making up for the lost time and frustrations of her youth, Marie did just that— with alacrity.

In 1957 Marie Stopes was diagnosed with cancer. Characteristic of her, she refused to believe the diagnosis; she went to Germany for specialized treatment, all to no avail. She died on October 2, 1958. She was cremated, and her ashes were scattered into the sea from a cliff by her son Harry and her most recent lover, Avro Manhattan. She was eulogized by the archdeacon of Westminster Cathedral, Dr. Adam Fox:

> It fell to her what falls to few of us, to espouse a cause which was strange to most, and shocking to many, and to see it at last generally accepted without protest and widely adopted as a matter of practice . . . Those who felt the impact of that personality will find themselves missing her ever and anon, believing it impossible that so much vitality should be lost or wasted.[9]

3

Feminist

In one sense, feminism is the least remarkable aspect of Marie Stopes' psychological makeup. As her friend and biographer Aylmer Maude recounts, "Her father, always anxious that she should not do things in a 'ladylike' way, taught the girl when and how to use screws instead of nails, and how to mitre a corner in making cabinets and shelves . . ."[10] In addition, as stated earlier, her mother Charlotte Carmichael was committed to women's suffrage, to opening educational and professional opportunity to women, and to various other *public* aspects of feminism— for example her work with the Rational Dress Society. For all that she might be said to have imbibed a disposition to feminism with her mother's milk, the feminism of Marie Stopes was of a very different cast than that of Charlotte Carmichael.

Where her mother focused exclusively on the *public* aspects of the feminist agenda, Marie focused in addition on the *private* aspects of feminism. The *very* private aspects. Indeed, in addition to advocating public policy on birth control and, later, eugenics, Marie brought a feminist awareness to the most intimate dimensions of human experience. Consider, for example, her discussion of the disparities in sexual appetite in men and women:

> If man's desire is perpetual and woman's intermittent; if man's desire naturally wells up every day or every few days, and woman's only every fortnight or every month, it may appear at first sight impossible for the unwarped needs of both natures simultaneously to be satisfied . . . The result has been that the supposed need of one of the partners has tended to become paramount, and we have established the social traditions of a husband's 'rights' and wifely 'duty'. As one man quite frankly said to me: 'As things are it is impossible for both sexes to get what they want. One *must* be sacrificed. And it is better for society that it should be the woman.'
> *Married Love,* p. 14

It is better for society that a woman's needs should be sacrificed? An *outrageous* assumption in Stopes' view— one that treats women as little more than an oversized erotic homunculus designed to service the sexual needs of men. It is an outlook that scripts a wife's "duty" as setting aside her own desires in favor of a husband's "right" to an uncomplicated orgasm. Here is the feminist revolution brought to the *sanctum sanctorum* of respectable society— the marriage bedroom. And for all that it is central to her feminism, I will defer elaboration of this aspect of her thought to my discussion of Marie Stopes as *Eroticist* in the next section of this introduction.

For now, I want to focus on another aspect of Stopes' feminism— one that triggered intense hostility from religious conservatives in Great Britain, and especially from the Roman Catholic Church. I refer to her strident advocacy of birth control. For many feminist thinkers of a century ago, it was clear that a consistent commitment to feminism entailed women taking control of their reproductive processes. Birth control was seen as inseparable from the feminist agenda for the simple reason that without the ability to control her own body, a woman could hardly be expected to control her own career, her professional destiny. And far more is at stake, in Stopes' view, than career opportunities for educated women.

Working women, especially those who are under-educated, who are living in poverty— these are among the most vulnerable people in society. And to keep information on contraception from such as these is to reduce their lot to abject desperation. Obviously more than one factor is keeping them locked in a cycle of misery, but chief among them is *ignorance*. In *Radiant Motherhood*, published in 1920, Stopes says:

> Often ignorance is blind and unaware that it is ignorance, stupidly blundering through life; but this is not always the mother's attitude. She may, indeed she often does, passionately desire knowledge and seek for it wherever she thinks she may find it in her restricted circle. Too tragically often she is baffled in her search. *Radiant Motherhood,* p. 72

Just this is what brought Marie Stopes and others, most notably Margaret Sanger in the United States, to disseminate information about both techniques and devices for contraception as widely as possible. Contraceptive devices were, at the time, typically sold by retailers who also merchandised pornography. Various models of condoms and diaphragms were collectively referred to, with some revulsion, as "rubber goods."

It was not Stopes' feminism, but her advocacy of birth control and contraception that brought on the hostile attentions of the Christian churches— most notably the

Roman Catholic Church— that generated the lawsuit that proved so distracting in Marie's career throughout most of the 1920's. Birth control was seen by the Christian establishment as a one-way street to social degeneration. It would undermine the basis of civilized behavior— sexual restraint. Knowledge of birth control, it was believed, was dangerous knowledge, most particularly for the lower classes. It would result in "copulation without consequences," a situation that would be especially ruinous to the undisciplined and under-educated poor in urban Britain.

It was just such attitudes that piqued Marie Stopes to impatience. If dangerous ignorance was at issue, she believed, the smug ignorance of the middle and upper classes about the plight of the impoverished women of their culture was also worthy of mention. Certainly she felt that the poor are in part responsible for their desperate circumstances; in an angry article in the *London Daily Mail* in 1919, she berated a fictional "Mrs. Jones" not for her lack of education, but for her lack of common sense. Equally problematic, she said in a 1931 speech, are those educated women who think that knowledge of birth control will only bring poor women to "be sent downhill on a life they ought not to embark upon." She dramatically illustrates her point from her own experience in running birth control clinics:

> The second person who came to my clinic when it first opened came on behalf of a girl of twenty who was pregnant for the sixth time! And every previous time she had had an abortion performed by her own mother! We, of course, had no help for that girl. We cannot deal with such cases. Yet it shows that in that terrible underworld of misery and anguish which we selfish, self-centered, lazy people so seldom visualise and understand, there *is* already 'knowledge' of a kind. 'Knowledge' is going round which is utterly detrimental, utterly unwholesome and tragic in its effects. The true

knowledge which we are bringing to counteract that is clean and wholesome . . .[11]

After years of having her science, her education, her patriotism, and her character excoriated by those claiming to represent the Christian teaching, she addressed herself to her Christian critics on their own terms. She challenged them to state whether or not the Bible, the divine law on which these Christians based their attacks, speaks to the issue of birth control:

> The wisdom of the Churches is ancient and pre-scientific: humanity to-day is modern and lives under increasingly "artificial" conditions: only the divinely-given everlasting truths are eternal, and on these the Churches must base their authority. Are any such divine laws given to the Churches about the Control of Conception?
> I answer—None. *Wise Parenthood,* p. 43

None. The holy writ is silent on the issue of contraception. And in a move of characteristic dash and audacity, Marie Stopes generously offered her services to remedy the situation. In 1920, two years after the publication of *Married Love* and *Wise Parenthood,* she published *A New Gospel for All the People.*

Christianity, like all monotheistic religions, purports to be a revealed religion. God, it is believed, reveals his will through human mouths: through Moses, Isaiah, and Jeremiah; through John the Baptist, Matthew, and Paul; through Muhammad. And, Marie Stopes announced, God had spoken again— this time through her. She was savvy enough not to be surprised by the guffaws she received from her co-religionists (throughout her life, Stopes considered herself a Christian), yet she was equally savvy in pointing out to them their inconsistency:

> While it is a fundamental tenet of the Christian Religion that
> the devout soul should be in a direct relation with God, yet it
> is strange that when this is true, astonishment and incredulity,
> rather than acceptance based on confirmatory experience, is
> usual. *A New Gospel for All the People*, p. 89

Stopes describes her revelation in phrases familiar to any
reader of the Bible. She tells us that she was aware of the
upcoming Conference of Anglican Bishops at Lambeth.
And, in her words—

> That week it chanced that I spent an afternoon alone in the
> cool shades of the old yew woods on the hills behind my
> home: While penetrated by that calm beauty there came,
> suddenly and quite explicitly, exact instructions in the words
> which follow. I was told: "Say to my Bishops"—what is found
> in these pages. At the conclusion of the message I arose and
> went home instantly; sent for my secretary; and there and then,
> without going into the house, redictated to him what had been
> dictated to me. *A New Gospel for All the People*, p. 90

Marie is on a roll. She steps into her religious persona
with theatrical flourish; clearly she has warmed to the idea of
prophesying to her Christian detractors. Continuing in a vein
that might have been taken from the Old Testament, she
advises the Bishops:

> To-day God sends a new revelation and a new Gospel.
> Hearken unto it. Harden not your hearts against the voice of
> God's revelation given in this present time. Say not among
> yourselves that God hath no more a living Prophet, and that
> nineteen centuries ago God spoke to humanity for the last
> time. *A New Gospel for All the People*, p. 94

What was Stopes actually thinking when she published *A
New Gospel for All the People?* Did she really think that
God had come down and spoken to her? Or— more

plausible in my view— had she adopted an antic disposition in which she meant to theatrically trump the traditional trump card of the Christian Churches, both Catholic and Protestant: "We speak in God's name"?

She understandably took the Churches to be the chief impediments to the revolution in thinking and social policy that she so urgently advocated. The Churches' trump card was, simply: We represent the word of God. *Thus saith the Lord.* But, claimed Marie, the Lord has spoken again, and He has spoken to *me*. And here's what He saith: *Take unto heart and implement the proposals of Dr. Marie Stopes.* Again, in her words: "Paul spoke with Christ nineteen hundred years ago. God spoke with me to-day." (*New Gospel,* p. 94)

It surprised no one, certainly not the Prophetess herself, that the Lambeth Conference did not scramble to accommodate itself to the new revelation. The Bishops pointedly rejected the central recommendations of Stopes' *A New Gospel.* In the Archives of the Lambeth Conferences, we find among the many Resolutions made by the Bishops at their 6th Conference of 1920, two that speak directly to the challenges posed by Marie Stopes:

Resolution 68

The Conference . . . regards with grave concern the spread in modern society of theories and practices hostile to the family. We utter an emphatic warning against the use of unnatural means for the avoidance of conception, together with the grave dangers— physical, moral and religious— thereby incurred, and against the evils with which the extension of such use threatens the race. In opposition to the teaching which, under the name of science and religion, encourages married people in the deliberate cultivation of sexual union as an end in itself, we steadfastly uphold what must always be regarded as the governing considerations of Christian marriage. One is the primary purpose for which marriage exists, namely the continuation of the race through the gift and heritage of children; the other is the paramount importance in married life of deliberate and thoughtful self-control.

Resolution 70

The Conference urges the importance of enlisting the help of all high-principled men and women, whatever be their religious beliefs, in co-operation with or, if necessary, in bringing pressure to bear upon, authorities both national and local, for removing such incentives to vice as indecent literature, suggestive plays and films, the open or secret sale of contraceptives, and the continued existence of brothels.[12]

Note that Resolution 70 places contraceptives among unsavory incentives like "indecent literature" and continued existence of brothels. Dirty books, whore-houses, and (although not mentioned by name) disgusting *rubber goods*— these are the legacy of birth control. In keeping with respectable attitudes of the times, the Lambeth Conference made a point of connecting birth control with obscenity and social degeneration.

The Bishops of the Conference were relatively circumspect in their rejection of Stopes' ideas. They rejected her ideas, but they remained aloof from responding to her claims to divine revelation. Not all respondents to *A New Gospel* were so diplomatic. One, Father F. M. De Zulueta, was far more direct in expressing his views:

I beg to acknowledge receipt of your pamphlet *[A New Gospel]* . . . Reading what you have put in cold print, I regard it as a most profane compound of imaginary mysticism and pornography. It may perhaps serve the purpose that type of young medical student who needs a veneer of religiosity to dignify his sexual pruriency, but could only revolt anyone with a real sense of religion— whether Catholic or non-Catholic.

I do not know on what ground you speak of your production as 'delivered' to the Lambeth Conference. At all events one would need to have stated the exact hour and date on which that assembly of gentlemen listened to the 'prophet' before regarding the description as anything more than a figure of speech.

But I know from some experience of life that when a woman gets to the point of saying 'I spoke to Christ yesterday' but has no idea of submitting her imagined inspirations to the judgment of any recognised spiritual authority, it is waste of time to reason. She is too self-satisfied to listen, much less to submit.

I remain, Madam, Yours obediently—[13]

Father De Zulueta suggests that in addition to "sexual pruriency," Marie is afflicted by the religious megalomania with which he is all too familiar. But he should have read her pamphlet more carefully. A careful reading of Stopes' text dispels the suspicion of undisciplined egotism that, at first blush, suggests itself. God, she tells us, speaks not so much through Marie Stopes, but through *science*. This is a point reasserted throughout the brief text. The "Word of God," we might say, is given to humanity through the *scientific method*. Marie really speaks for God indirectly— she presents herself as the voice of his authentic revelatory presence to humanity, *science*. What she is doing is something that anyone might do, and that in her view all of us should do: Try to understand the world and ourselves through science rather than through irrational hopes, superstition, and a dogmatic adherence to traditional authority.

What seems at first blush to be a puckish and defiant gesture in the face of church authorities appears, on closer consideration, to be an entirely serious call to the banner of the Enlightenment: "In the name of God, I call upon you Ministers of the Church to listen to *the revelations God makes through Science,* to listen to the extension of Christ's teaching . . ." (*A New Gospel for All the People,* p.102, emphasis added)

We read at Luke 4:24 "Truly, I say to you, no prophet is acceptable in his own country." Or in *her* own country, Marie would attest. I've already suggested that it is most unlikely that she seriously expected a mass conversion— that the Christian churches in Great Britain might take her Gospel at face value and piously adopt her views on sexuality and birth control. And yet it is equally unlikely that she was being entirely unserious and frivolous in writing *A New Gospel.* As we'll see in the section on Marie Stopes as *Eroticist,* sexuality was more than a social or biological issue for her; it was an intensely *spiritual* issue. As a religious woman and as a Christian, she intended her work as a correction to attitudes toward sexuality that had been endemic to the Christian tradition from its earliest centuries. Such attitudes are found in the views of the ancient Church Father, Clement of Alexandria. In her popular book *Adam, Eve, and the Serpent,* the historian Elaine Pagels tells us of Clements's pronouncements on sexuality:

> To engage in marital intercourse for any other reason [than procreation] is to "do injury to nature." Clement excludes not only such counterproductive practices as oral and anal intercourse but also intercourse with a menstruating, pregnant, barren, or menopausal wife, and, for that matter, with one's wife "in the morning," "in the daytime," or "after dinner." Clement warns, indeed, that "not even at night, although in darkness, is it fitting to carry on immodestly or indecently, but with modesty, so that whatever happens, happens in the light of reason . . . for even that union which is legitimate is still dangerous, except in so far as it is engaged in procreation of children."[14]

It is worth repeating that Stopes was a deeply religious person, and that she saw herself as a Christian. As a Christian and a feminist, she— like feminists of the late 20th and early 21st centuries— felt compelled to challenge the institutionalized Church view that sexuality serves the purely instrumental purpose of reproduction and is not of intrinsic value in itself.

Whether the promotion of a healthy, sacramental attitude toward human sexuality is disparaged by the Bishops of the Lambeth Conference (who oppose the teaching that "under the name of science and religion encourages married people in the deliberate cultivation of sexual union as an end in itself") or by the hoary ancient source of Clement of Alexandria (who after his round-the-clock prohibitions declared that "even that union which is legitimate is still dangerous, except in so far as it is engaged in procreation of children")— the status of sexuality is profaned.

And at least to those who think like Marie Stopes, the results are predictable. The disparagement of sexuality doesn't evaporate sexual desire. And in an institution like the Christian Church, no matter if Catholic or Protestant, that is governed all but exclusively by men, it should surprise no one that responsibility for the stubborn persistence of sexual distraction (if that's what it is) will be laid at the feet of *women.* That is why for Marie Stopes, as for later feminists, women's liberation entailed religious reformation.

We'll return to these aspects of Stopes' thought in due course. For now, there's another aspect of her feminism that is relevant to understanding her strident advocacy of birth control. The trajectory of society was tending toward disaster, as Stopes saw it. Without the implementation of rational contraception policies, social chaos was inevitable. The concern here is with the state of society, not the state of the species; at issue is politics— not, at this point at least, eugenics. Stopes' concern about eugenics will be considered in the next section.

For now, our focus is on Stopes' concern that the stability of society is menaced by uncontrolled reproduction— from a lack of birth control. In *Radiant Motherhood,* she states her conviction that social chaos and revolution is brewing in English society. Speaking of the mindset characteristic of those advocating an overthrow of the social order, she reports that:

> In effect they say: "Society has starved us, given us bad conditions." Thus they foster a grievance against "society" in their minds. One bitter leader said to me:—
>
>> I was one of fourteen children, and my mother had only a little three-roomed cottage near Glasgow. We nearly starved when I was young. I know what the poor suffer at the hands of society.
>>
>> . . .This country, and nearly all the world, has innumerable homes in which the seed of revolution is sown in myriads of minds from the moment they are conceived. Revolted, horrorstricken mothers bear children whose coming birth they fear. A starved, stunted outlook is stamped upon their brains and bodies in the most intimate manner before they come into the world, so oriented towards it that they must run counter to the healthy, happy constructive stream of human life. *Radiant Motherhood,* p. 66-67

A public policy that actively supports contraception is not just a *good* course of action in the moral sense, it is an eminently *practical* strategy. Stopes urgently proposes birth control as an insurance policy against the destructive processes of revolution and social upheaval. Put otherwise, what is good for women, collectively and individually, is also good for society. Marie Stopes was not alone in this thinking. In America, Margaret Sanger, who had served as an early inspiration for Marie, wrote this:

> What shall be done? We have our choice of one of three policies. We may abandon our science and leave the weak and diseased to die, or kill them, as the brutes do. Or we may go on overpopulating the earth and have our famines and our wars while the earth exists. Or we can accept the third, sane,

sensible, moral and practicable plan of birth control. We can
refuse to bring weak, the helpless and the unwanted children
into the world. We can refuse to overcrowd families, nations
and the earth. There are these ways to meet the situation, and
only these three ways.[15]

The rational planning of families is not a totalitarian
policy that will need to be inflicted on the lower classes—
poor women may be uneducated, but they do not lack a
desire for a dignified life. It takes no sophisticated grasp of
economics to understand the connections between poverty
and unrestrained childbirth; it takes no medical degree to
appreciate the health consequences of getting pregnant while
still nursing an infant.

Stopes collected an extensive amount of personal
testimony from women of all classes in interviews she
conducted in the various birth control clinics she had
established, from casual conversations with women in
neighborhood surveys, and from the vast correspondence she
received as the acknowledged doyen of birth control in Great
Britain. Her social research brought her to conclusions that
sound naïve to many of us in the 21st century; they are
optimistic and idealistic to the point of utopianism:

> When once the women of *all* classes have the fear and dread
> of undesired maternity removed from them, they will be free
> to put all their delicate strength into creating desired and
> beautiful children. And it is on the feet of those children that
> the race will go forward into the promised land of Utopia.
> "The Control of Parenthood: Imperial and Racial Aspects," p.
> 112

It was Stopes' sincere belief that contraception is the
royal road to the improvement of life for all classes—
wealthy, middle-class, and working-class. And this was true,
she believed, for none more than the working classes.
Feminism, in her view, was never just about women. And as

we'll see in what follows, Stopes' vision of feminism is not just about her own society, Great Britain. Nor is her vision of feminism just about Western civilization. Feminism, in Stopes' view, is ultimately about the human species— it is about the species' future thriving; it is about the very survival of the species.

4

Eroticist

> "The past is another country: they do things differently there."
> L. P. Hartley, *The Go-Between*

Recently, while browsing in a huge Barnes and Noble bookstore, I came across a book titled *The Complete Idiot's Guide to Amazing Sex,* written by Sari Locker. Like other books in *The Complete Idiot's Guide* series, it is succinct, well-written, and entertaining. On page 165, in a chapter titled "Reach Out and Touch Someone," there is the following advice on arousing a woman to sexual passion:

—Be careful with the sensitive clitoris. Some women don't like continuous direct stimulation of their clitoris because it is too sensitive. Unless she tells you she enjoys direct stimulation, you can rub on top of her clitoral hood (the skin that covers the clitoris), or alternately rub the clitoris and the area around the clitoris.

—Rub around the vagina and labia. Rub with one or two of your fingers up and down the opening between her labia, on her labia, and around her vagina.

—Slip a finger or two into her vagina. Some women like to have their vagina penetrated with one or more fingers. A woman might like it when you rub the upper, inner wall of her vagina, where the mysterious G-spot is located (see Chapter 8 for information on the G-spot).[16]

And so on. And on much further. The reader is likely to be familiar, at least in a cursory way, with such intimate instruction. It is readily available and is, for most of us in the 21st century, entirely unremarkable. This text of husky advice is not locked away; it is displayed with other self-help books. Ms. Locker's book is clearly not seen as particularly *hot* or shocking. When I paid for it at the checkout register, there were no blushes, no knowing glances. A thoroughly blasé transaction— which is exactly as it should be. But it should not escape us that, during the first decades of the 20th century, *The Complete Idiot's Guide to Amazing Sex* would have been condemned as pornographic and a threat to public morality. Copies of the book would have been legally confiscated and, in all likelihood, the bookseller would have been arrested.

For better and for worse, we live in a world that has been significantly configured by Marie Stopes. Candid talk about sexual details is now the norm— it is taken to be realistic and healthy. There is little doubt that such candor is healthy. That's the "for better" side of the equation. But the move toward sexual explicitness also laid the groundwork for abandoning almost any control over sexually explicit material (except that involving children). One needn't be a prudish Victorian to be dismayed by the flood of raunchy pornography that pervades the internet. This, for many, is the "for worse" side of the equation. Marie Stopes' biographer, Ruth Hall, describes the attitudes toward sexuality—

attitudes entirely representative of the time— in which Marie's mother Charlotte was raised:

> Charlotte, in common with most women of her class, knew nothing about sex when she married. The subject was never discussed. It was the white woman's burden, an indignity to be stoically endured in order to achieve the righteous goals of producing children and satisfying a husband whose sexual needs were different from her own. The virtuous wife, as the few marriage manuals pointed out, "submitted" unwillingly to her husband but— far from demanding satisfaction— was expected to feel ashamed should she experience any sexual gratification.[17]

An indignity to be stoically endured. And this was not an exclusively European disposition. In Thornton Wilder's 1938 Pulitzer Prize winning play, *Our Town,* there is a wedding dramatized in Act II. One of the older characters witnessing the ceremony, Mrs. Webb, turns suddenly and speaks directly to the audience:

> Oh, I've got to say it: you know, there's something downright cruel about sending our girls out into marriage this way. I hope some of her girl friends have told her a thing or two. It's cruel, I know, but I couldn't bring myself to say anything. I went into it blind as a bat myself.[18]

Deep ignorance about the details of human sexuality is sometimes the material for jokes. In real life, however, it is anything but funny. As we've already seen, few knew this better than Marie Stopes herself. It needs no ghost of Dr. Freud to tell us that our sexual life— our *erotic* life, not just our reproductive life— is central to human well-being. In a culture in which *The Complete Idiot's Guide to Amazing Sex* is a commonplace in mainstream bookstores (as opposed to back-alley pornography shops), it is difficult to imagine that there was a time when a devastating ignorance was the general rule regarding sexuality and the erotic.

It was into this psycho-social milieu that Marie Stopes launched her own version of feminism. Recall that her mother Charlotte Carmichael Stopes was herself an ardent feminist. But the feminism of her mother's generation was deeply suspicious of sensuality. When Marie's advocacy of the sexual dimensions of her understanding of feminism became public, one of her mother's friends wrote her in alarm: "Once let that sex feeling run only in the sensual channel and we, as a Nation, are done for."[19] Marie was first and foremost an ardent feminist. Like other feminists of her day, she stridently called attention to the political implications of feminism. Unlike most other feminists of her day, she asserted what she took to be the *sexual* core of the feminism. For Stopes, the task was to bring the *whole woman* into the feminist agenda. The inclusion of women in professional life that requires of those women that they "unsex" themselves is *not* an authentic feminism. Sexuality, for Stopes, is where feminist theory actually comes to *life*. Without being embodied through the core of a woman's being, her sexuality, feminism remains no more than a theoretical abstraction— an employment opportunity, no more. And when Stopes published *Married Love* in 1918, she presented what might be called an erotic manifesto. She did not tip-toe. Here is a representative passage from Chapter 5:

> What actually happens in an act of union should be known. After the preliminaries have mutually roused the pair, the stimulated penis, enlarged and stiffened, is pressed into the woman's vagina. Ordinarily when a woman is not stimulated, the walls of this canal, as well as the exterior lips of soft tissue surrounding it, are dry and rather crinkled, and the vaginal opening is smaller than the man's extended penis. But when the woman is what is physiologically called tumescent (that is,

when she is ready for union and has been profoundly stirred) these parts are flushed by the internal blood supply and to some extent are turgid like those of the man, while a secretion of mucous lubricates the channel of the vagina. In an ardent woman the vagina may even spontaneously open and close. (*Married Love,* p. 20-21)

While decent people in Stopes' time were shocked and indignant, today her relentless explicitness may evoke a condescending smile— what, really, was the big deal? It is most important to remember that this question is asked in a culture in which Locker's *The Complete Idiot's Guide to Amazing Sex* is unremarkable. In fact, Stopes' publication of *Married Love* was a *very* big deal for those mired in ignorance, for those in pain and confusion over issues that they barely dared *think* about, much less *talk* about. Again, we forget how truly different the world of only a generation or two in the past can be from our own. And so we are bemused by the fact that, in 1918, Stopes' writings on sexuality in *Married Love* evoked outrage.

Marie Stopes was no fool. The hostile response from much of the press did not take her by surprise. What surprised her, and dismayed many who were horrified by her approach, was the positive response to *Married Love* across a large segment of the population. In today's terms, *Married Love* would be called a runaway bestseller. In Ruth Hall's biography, we read that—

In 1935 a number of American academics were asked to list the twenty-five most influential books of the previous fifty years. Their findings were collated and in the final list *Married Love* was accorded sixteenth place out of the twenty-five— just behind *Das Kapital, The Golden Bough,* and Havelock Ellis' *Psychology of Sex,* but ahead of Einstein's *Relativity,* Freud's *Interpretation of Dreams,* Hitler's *Mein Kampf,* and Keynes's *Economic Consequences* of the Peace.[20]

According to her friend and biographer Aylmer Maude, she did not anticipate such a sunny reception of her work— to say it again, she was *surprised*. Describing Stopes' state of mind at the time when *Married Love* was published, Maude tells us that "She was quite prepared to be imprisoned. The one thing she was not prepared for was the avalanche of thanks and gratitude, the thousands and tens of thousands of touching letters that inundated her from all parts of the world."[21] And these tens of thousands of letters betokened a galloping publication success— a success that all but swamped the capacities of her first publisher, A. C. Fifield. In her biographical study, June Rose offers a perceptive account of the phenomenon:

> The reasons for its success are complex. Writing from a woman's point of view, with an intensity of feeling with which many readers would empathize, Marie had produced the first book about sex technique for women. In it she had dared to stake a claim for female sexuality, for women's sexual needs and sexual rights. Her views challenged the centuries of prejudice and superstition and the accretions of religious teaching which saw women's bodies and women's attractions as desirable but also dirty and corrupting and the lust for women as shameful and sinful. The wife's fate, therefore, was to be a passive suffering victim of her husband's lust. Marie dismissed the idea that 'nice' women have no spontaneous sexual impulses and devoted a chapter . . . to explaining women's sexual instincts . . .[22]

The full story of the reception of *Married Love* is still more complex. The human engagement of sexuality has never been straightforward. And in the early decades of the 20th century, feelings were more conflicted than usual because cultural change regarding sexuality was proceeding at a rapid pace. And, it is important to note, there was no clear consensus among those women who identified themselves as feminists. Thinking was sometimes unscientific, sometimes outright irrational. Even purportedly *scientific* outlooks appear, from a 21st century perspective, to be a species of pseudoscience. Yes, the Freudian revolution in psychology had been underway since 1900, but that discussion was typically restricted to academics and medical professionals. When details of Freud's theories reached the general public, the clinical and philosophical tone in which they were presented made them seem alien and even forbidding. The great appeal of Stopes' writings on sexuality— especially for women— is that she spoke directly from intimate experience, from an experience with which other women could readily identify.

But the sensuality so vigorously endorsed by Stopes was not a disposition with which most feminists resonated. This may sound odd to us today, but a hundred years ago many feminists saw sexuality as a *trap*. And there were good reasons for that. Given the prevailing attitudes both toward sexuality and toward women, perhaps the feminists of a century ago despaired— again, for good reasons— that there could be a sexual relation to men in which their rights and human dignity could be maintained. Perhaps we see evidence of how powerful social conditioning can be, in this case conditioning to the idea that respectable women did not enjoy sex, that a "lady" submitted to the brute necessities of sexuality for the sake of reproduction as a lamentable duty. It was perhaps easy for the burgeoning feminist consciousness to assume that the sex act was inherently debasing, and that sexual hunger— especially on the part of a woman— was a mark of moral depravity.

This view was prominently represented in eminent turn of the century feminists like Elizabeth Cady Stanton, Susan B. Anthony, Charlotte Perkins Gilman, and many others. For these women, the issue of "female sexuality" was deeply conflicted. No doubt this reflects more than a political strategy. In her autobiographical study, *The Living of Charlotte Perkins Gilman*, Gilman makes clear that for all her forceful assertion of gender equality, she conceived that equality in terms of a commitment to *chastity*, not eroticism. Here's how she puts it:

> Perhaps the most salient change of the present period is the lowering of standards in sex relations, approaching some of the worst periods in ancient history. In my youth there was a fine, earnest movement toward an equal standard of chastity for men and women, an equalizing upward to the level of what women were then. But now the very word "chastity" seems to have become ridiculous.[23]

Gilman's model of gender equality in regard to sexuality is one in which men would be raised to the higher standards maintained by women— not one in which women would be lowered to the animality of male sexual appetite. In another passage from her autobiography, Gilman tells us that she was not unaware of the Freudian revolution— on the contrary, she says, with a twinge of resignation, that "unfortunately my views on the sex question do not appeal to the Freudian complex of today . . ."[24] Elaborating on this trend, historian George Robb says:

> Many 19th-century utopians believed that the sexual subordination of women would only disappear if society were somehow rendered 'sexless'. During the 1880s the Theosophical Society. . . began a long association with English feminism. Theosophy appealed to feminists through its emphasis on the equality of the sexes, the motherhood of God, and an evolutionary pattern that promised to transcend differentiated sexuality. . . Theosophists saw human evolution as a grand cosmic procession in which the Darwinian ascent of man from ape was but a tiny segment. . . In 1884 the spiritualist Laurence Oliphant published *Sympneumata*, a book

widely read, in which he foresaw a future androgynous society where children would be created non-sexually. Theosophists in particular anticipated the creation of a higher being that would free humanity from sex altogether. Writing in *The Theosophist* in 1914, Susan Gay held that the future race would reproduce parthenogenically.[25]

Parthenogenically— that is, by way of virgin birth. The hope was that evolution would follow a trajectory beyond the material, beyond gross physicality, to a *spiritual* plane. Recourse to such pre-scientific thinking was, improbable as it seems to the modern mind, a popular idea among feminists of a century ago. One example of this desperate hope is found in Charlotte Perkins Gilman's most famous work, her 1915 utopian novel *Herland*. Describing a remote island on which human life evolved exclusively through women, Gilman presents this situation:

> For five or ten years they worked together, growing stronger and wiser and more and more mutually attached, and then the miracle happened— one of these young women bore a child. Of course they all thought there must be a man somewhere, but none was found. Then they decided it must be a direct gift from the gods, and placed the proud mother in the Temple of Maaia— their Goddess of Motherhood— under strict watch. And there, as years passed, this wonder-woman bore child after child, five of them, all girls. . . As fast as they reached the age of twenty-five they began bearing. Each of them, like her mother, bore five daughters. Presently there were twenty-five New Women, Mothers in their own right, and the whole spirit of the country changed from mourning and mere courageous resignation to proud joy. The older women, those who remembered men, died off; the youngest of all the first lot of course died too, after a while, and by that time there were left one hundred and fifty-five parthenogenetic women, founding a new race.[26]

No doubt it was Marie Stopes' scientific training that kept her from such unscientific models. In developing her own views, she was influenced by the thinking of the pioneer sexologist who, in fact, preceded Sigmund Freud— Havelock Ellis. Stopes was highly selective in her use of Ellis, and with good reason. Ellis' monumental *Studies in the Psychology of Sex,* published in six volumes between 1897 and 1910, is a revolutionary attempt to place human sexuality within the context of evolutionary biology. By today's standards, much of Ellis' treatment of female sexuality in particular seems ham-handed and loutish.[27] But a century ago his theories, called the "sexological" approach, were influential— at least among intellectuals. When Marie Stopes popularized such discourse, she emphasized Ellis' naturalistic claims, and she emphasized his insistence that women are as libidinous as men. But because she believed that women should *control* the sexual relationship, she rejected passages like this one from the third volume of Ellis' study:

> This association between love and pain still persists even among the most normal civilized men and women possessing well-developed sexual impulses. The masculine tendency to delight in domination, the feminine tendency to delight in submission, still maintain the ancient traditions when the male animal pursued the female. . . To exert power, as psychologists well recognize, is one of our most primary impulses, and it always tends to be manifested in the attitude of a man toward the woman he loves.[28]

Another idea taken by Stopes from Havelock Ellis was the theory of "seminal absorption." According to this theory— now discredited— women not only obtain children through sexual intercourse, they attain *vital nutrients.* Through the vaginal absorption of semen, women gain access to what they need for both physical and psychological health. According to Ellis: "It is due to this influence. . . that weak and anemic girls so often become full-blooded and robust after marriage, and lose their nervous tendencies and shyness."[29] Here's how the idea finds expression in Stopes' *Enduring Passion:*

> I have come to the conclusion that there undoubtedly is a real physiological hunger for the chemical and complex molecular substances found in the accessory glands of the male, which can be supplied to women who unconsciously feel their need and show it in the apparently irrelevant but really quite direct way of inviting sex union in what appears excessive amounts from their mates. Or, sometimes, from lovers in addition to their husbands. *Enduring Passion*, p. 131

Stopes' endorsement of the seminal absorption theory served to situate her sexual theories within a naturalist context, thereby conferring a "scientific" realism on them. But there were also disadvantages. The cheerful message that men are possessed of vital fluids was tempered by the belief that the reservoir of these fluids is *finite.* That is, male vitality is not inexhaustible. The more a man "contributed" to his wife, the less he had for himself. The idea of women taking essential nutrition from male fluids was, in the popular mind, morphed into an image of women feeding on men. *Vampire!*

In 1897 Bram Stoker published his novel *Dracula*— a story about vampires, about entities who *feed* on humans— a story that both reflected and abetted the sense of dread that was emerging in regard to female sexuality. Stopes was clearly aware of these developments, and her confrontational disposition brought her to publically defy them. In her 1931 book, *Enduring Passion,* she reports on an indignant male reader's reaction to her earlier book, *Married Love:*

> Few men are quite as frank as was Lord X. Before I wrote this book [that is, *Enduring Passion]*, when in the privacy of a

tête-à-tête in his own house, he turned upon me with bitterness for having told womanhood in my book *Married Love* of the physical joys of marriage. "What have you done?" he exclaimed. "You have broken up the home; you have let women know about things which only prostitutes ought to know; once you give women a taste for these things, they become vampires, and you have let loose vampires into decent men's homes. . . We do not want that sort of thing in our own homes. The wife should be the housekeeper and make the home a place of calm comfort for a man. Instead of that you have made my home a hell: I cannot meet the demands of my wife now she knows. If you create these vampire women, you will rear a race of effeminate men." *Enduring Passion,* p. 124-125

Admittedly, this account is related by Stopes herself, not the worried husband she calls Lord X. But "Lord X" is not a caricature; the concerns to which he gives voice were concerns that radiated through the general population of Europe of a century ago. In a perceptive and readable study titled *Evil Sisters: the Threat of Female Sexuality and the Cult of Manhood,* historian Bram Dijkstra discusses these anxieties at length. He describes how such folktales and pseudoscience could crystallize into dark suspicions:

The analogue between the girl next door and the vampires who were . . . held to account in folklore for wasting diseases as tuberculosis, became frighteningly direct if a man's stock of vitality must diminish in proportion to the manner in which, as Ellis put it, "weak and anemic girls" became "full-blooded and robust after marriage." Clearly the continuous depletion of that tonic that made the girl next door into a strapping physical specimen must have just the opposite on the donor and was bound to turn him, like the vampire victim in days of yore, into a tubercular wreck.[30]

A final voice on the issue of seminal absorption needs to be considered to convey a sense of the motley variety of attitudes that had their moment in the European culture of a century ago, the stage onto which Stopes brought her erotic revolution.

A variation on the theme of seminal absorption was provided by the idiosyncratic feminist Frances Swiney (1847-1922). An adherent to the Theosophical movement, Swiney is little-known today except among historians, but during her life she was an influential and prolific writer on women's rights. At the end of her life, in 1921, Swiney corresponded briefly with Marie Stopes, but the distance between their outlooks on sexuality may be gauged by Swiney's position on seminal absorption. In her 1909 book, *The Bar of Isis: the Law of the Mother,* Swiney presents her view that, far from being nutritive, semen is a source of pollution and disease— a genuine menace to the woman exposed to it. With a thrill of revulsion, she tells us that "All seminal fluid, being of the nature of excreta, decomposes in the system of the woman." And the presence of this decomposing seminal fluid is anything but benign. She continues:

> To show its virulence, Dr. J. H. Tressel writes: "I took decomposed human generative fluid and injected it into the vascular system of guinea-pigs and rabbits. The most of them died within twenty-four hours. I also took the fluid of putrid meat and tried it in the same manner, but found that it was not so deadly as the semen; it proved to be a much less active poison. Some of the animals did not die from the effects of the putrid meat infection, and those which did [not] lived longer than any inoculated with the spermatozoic poison." —See *Modern Researches,* p. 269[31]

Clearly Swiney's views sound extreme in the 21st century— unscientific and even pathological. Running directly counter to the views of Ellis, and later Freud, and still later Marie Stopes, Swiney insisted that physical sexuality was not natural because it served the agenda of male dominance. Again, historian George Robb states the case succinctly: "In a startling transvaluation of values, Swiney was contesting her society's definition of 'natural.' Sexual desire, even for men, was not natural. In particular, the male dominance of society was unnatural."[32] Radical and idiosyncratic, no doubt— but Swiney's attitudes were not *outré* in her day, especially among feminists. We've already seen how Charlotte Perkins Gilman enthused over the possibility of parthenogenesis. Helena Petrovna Blavatsky, the guiding spirit of the Theosophy movement, lamented the brute physicality of the reproductive processes in these words: ". . .by turning the holy mysteries of procreation into animal gratification. . . man became. . . a helpless, scrofulous being. . . the most consciously and intelligently bestial of all animals!"[33]

But for Stopes, not a spiritual transcendence, but a spiritual *embracement* of physicality was the ideal. The mysteries of procreation— replete with "animal gratification"— are capable of expressing a conscious participation in the divine. In *Married Love,* she describes sexuality in terms that are indisputably religious, as a unique path to a mystical experience that is attainable only through the reciprocal experience of two people joined in love. She says:

> . . . One might compare two human beings to two bodies charged with electricity of different potentials. Isolated from each other the electric forces within them are invisible, but if they come into the right juxtaposition the force is transmuted, and a spark, a glow of burning light arises between them. Such is love. From the body of the loved one's simple, sweetly coloured flesh, which our immemorial creature instincts urge us to desire, there springs not only the wonder of a new bodily life, but also the enlargement of the horizon of human sympathy and the glow of spiritual understanding which a

solitary soul could never have attained alone. *Married Love,*
p. 7-8

Where many of her fellow-feminists were repulsed by
the physicality of reproduction, Stopes was repulsed by the
factors that evoked that repulsion. She was repulsed by the
male-centered model of sexuality that prevailed in her
culture, a model in which it was the lamentable duty of a
wife to provide accommodation of male sexual hunger. This
model relegated women, as stated above, to the status of an
oversized sexual homunculus designed to service male
needs. But Stopes took the indignation felt by so many other
feminists, however understandable it was, to be misdirected.
For Stopes, the problem was not sexuality itself, but a
catastrophically *unbalanced understanding* of sexuality. As
we've seen, the unique sexual needs of women were first
disparaged and then righteously ignored— after all, "ladies"
were not possessed of such needs. The healthy sexuality
proposed by Stopes would be *reciprocal,* not symmetrical
(women had different sexual needs than men). Her proposals
were met with horror by most conventional people of her
day. And as we've just seen, they were with the views of
most feminists of her day— women as diverse in disposition
as Helena Blavatsky, Frances Swiney, and Charlotte Perkins
Gilman.

The reaction against Stopes' eroticist agenda went
further than disapproval. Across the Atlantic, her books were
legally banned. Under the 1873 Comstock Law it was
illegal— and punishable by up to five years at hard labor in
the penitentiary— to produce, sell, or possess "an obscene
book, pamphlet, paper, writing, advertisement, circular,
print, picture, drawing . . . or other article of an immoral
nature . . . or any article whatever, for the prevention of
conception, or for causing unlawful abortion."[34] Stopes'
Married Love was deemed to fall within the purview of this
law; it was classified as obscene book and hence a threat to

public order. This ruling on the book stayed in force until 1931, when the U. S. Supreme Court ruled that *Married Love* was not obscene and should be allowed for sale in the United States.

It is inevitable, perhaps, to speculate that the centrality of sexuality to the feminist agenda of Marie Stopes is rooted in her biography— in the bitter frustrations she experienced in her youth and especially in her first marriage. No doubt these frustrations provided some of the spark in her advocacy. But to assume that it tells the whole story would be rash. Stopes vision for everything she advocated was passionate and, for lack of a better word, *embodied.* She had little use for the merely theoretical. As she confided in a letter to her friend Aylmer Maude in 1915, before her public career had been launched—

> More and more intensely do I feel that the one thing worth bringing into and trying to increase in the world is love, love and its joy and beauty in every form and every possible expression. That is why I am beginning to revolt against so much of the so-called 'intellectual' work. . .[35]

The problem with merely "intellectual" work, for Stopes, is that it too easily left behind the realities of the street— the realities of life. An authentic feminism entailed practical, embodied realities. An authentic feminism embraced, without embarrassment, a vibrant and healthy sensuality.

Certainly, for Stopes, feminism without an erotic dimension was desiccated and bloodless. But there was more at stake, and here we begin to segue to another dimension of Marie Stopes' writings. We've seen that in her view, feminism without knowledge of and broad access to the techniques of birth control was an empty gesture. And access to birth control must not be restricted to the privileged classes; it was imperative, for Stopes, that the impoverished and ill-educated segments of society be empowered to control their reproduction. In her irascible article in the *London Daily Mail,* Stopes not only accuses the fictional "Mrs. Jones" of personal irresponsibility, but also scolds British culture itself as complicit in the wretched destitution of Mrs. Jones. "She needed the knowledge of what is called 'birth control' to begin with. Why did she not have it? Echo answers, because of our national stupidity, prudery, and barbarism." ("How Mrs. Jones Does Her Worst," p. 115) Stopes saw the same *prudery* that stood aghast at her erotic proclamations to be operative in bourgeois reservations that access to birth control would be morally ruinous to the lower classes— that "copulation without consequences" would undermine the sexual restraint indispensible to civilization.

But again, there's more to the story. There are also *responsibilities* entailed in the broad dissemination of the knowledge of birth control. It quickly became clear to feminists on both sides of the Atlantic that the successful implementation of birth control would have *demographic* impact. The feminists of a century ago were typically committed to the idea that feminism was about more than women's rights. The feminist agenda, they believed, was a blueprint both for the enhancement of society and of human nature. It was this belief that brought most feminists to advocate eugenics. And it is to this aspect of Marie Stopes' thought that we now turn.

5

Eugenicist

For all her advocacy of birth control, Stopes was not concerned with the general issue of over-population. She was concerned with over-population among specific groups of people— namely, those people who cannot afford children or who should not have children. In a BBC interview in September of 1957 (a year before her death), Stopes said this:

> It doesn't matter to me how many people there are in the world so long as they're first-rate in quality. We wouldn't have any of the troubles we have at present if everybody was first-rate in quality and you can only get first-rate quality by having proper application of birth control . . . We are breeding rubbish . . . we are educating rubbish, and this lack of self-discipline, the lack of common honesty in young people— appalls me.[36]

This concern for *quality,* a concern taken to be implicit in the dynamics of the feminist agenda, led Marie Stopes and many other feminists to be stanch advocates of eugenics. While she stood alone in her assertion of the erotic core of feminism, Stopes' commitment to eugenics as an essential feature of feminist theory was all but universal among feminists of her day. More than intellectually sound, eugenics was taken to be *common sense.* Today, Stopes' eroticism is taken to be common sense; it is the eugenic aspects of her writing that is taken to be scandalous. Some historical background is in order.

The word eugenics is taken from the Greek: *eu-genesis* = "good breeding." Eugenics is a common practice among ranchers and plant breeders: it is selective breeding. Selective breeding is the process through which we have nourishing corn with large ears and big kernels; it is the process by which we have beef cattle with great muscle bulk; it is the process that gave us the Chihuahua dog. And just that horrifies many: it takes an "improvement of the breed" approach to make better corn and cows and dogs— and applies it to humans.

Eugenics is not a new idea. The hope to improve humanity by enhancing both the *quantity* and the *quality* of the most gifted among us, is central to the political philosophy of Plato. He sets forth a program of "selective breeding" for humanity in Book V of his most famous work, the *Republic.* Here's how he puts it:

> Tell me this, Glaucon. I see that you have in your house hunting dogs and a number of pedigreed cocks. Have you ever considered something about their unions and procreations? [What? he said.]
> In the first place, I said, among these themselves, although they are a select breed, do not some prove better than the rest? [They do.]
> Do you then breed from all indiscriminately, or are you careful to breed from the best? [From the best.] . . .
> . . . How imperative, then, is our need of the highest skill in our rulers, if the principle holds also for mankind . . . It follows from our former admissions, I said, that the best men must cohabit with the best women in as many cases as possible and the worst with the worst in the fewest, and that the offspring of the one must be reared and that of the other not, if the flock is to be as perfect as possible. And the way in which all this is brought to pass must be unknown to any but the rulers, if, again, the herd of guardians is to be as free as possible from dissension. *Republic* 459a-e (Shorey translation)

The dynamics of the agenda presented by Plato can be stated succinctly: like produces like; maximize the breeding of the good stock; minimize the breeding of the bad stock. At its most basic, eugenics is not, as we might say today, rocket science. But it *is* science. That is, eugenics, as Plato presents it, calls for the systematic application of a *method* for improving the human stock. And some twenty-two centuries after Plato wrote the *Republic,* the concern for a quality of human breeding was once again a matter of serious discussion.

The modern emergence of eugenics is associated with the theories of Francis Galton (1822-1911)— a cousin of Charles Darwin. Although Galton is taken to be the originator of modern eugenic theory (he coined the term "eugenics"), in fact he was preceded by his more illustrious cousin. Throughout his historic 1859 work, *The Origin of Species by Means of Natural Selection*, Darwin asserts the view that all life forms, including the human, develop the capacity to survive and maintain their survival by facing the merciless rigors of natural selection— a process whereby the least fit are weeded out, the more fit survive and thrive, and therefore reproduce themselves disproportionately. In Chapter 5 of *The Descent of Man* (1871), he famously applies the principle to humans and human society:

> With savages, the weak in body or mind are soon eliminated; and those that survive commonly exhibit a vigorous state of health. We civilized men, on the other hand, do our utmost to check the process of elimination; we build asylums for the imbecile, the maimed, and the sick; we institute poor-laws; and our medical men exert their utmost skill to save the life of every one to the last moment . . . It is surprising how soon a want of care, or care wrongly directed, leads to the degeneration of a domestic race; but excepting in the case of man himself, hardly any one is so ignorant as to allow his worst animals to breed.[37]

In this important passage, Darwin reasserts the concerns spoken of so long ago by Plato: a concern both that the best be encouraged to reproduce, and that the worst be discouraged from doing so. Darwin restates the ancient concern with both eugenics and its opposite, *dysgenics*— from the Greek for bad (*dys*) breeding. Although he refers to them as "savages," he obviously recommends the practice of those cultures that discourage the reproduction of their least-promising members; the methods may be harsh, but the practice insures against the "degeneration of the stock."

Neither Plato nor Darwin used the word "eugenics." That word was coined, as stated above, by Darwin's cousin, Francis Galton. In his 1883 book, *Inquiries into Human Faculty and Its Development,* in writing of the cultivation of the human race, he advocated: ". . . what is termed in Greek, *eugenes* namely, good in stock, hereditarily endowed with noble qualities. This, and the allied words, *eugeneia*, etc., are equally applicable to men, brutes, and plants."[38] Despite the disquieting inclusion of humans among the "brutes and plants" that provide the material for eugenic experimentation, the intellectual world of the first decade of the 20th century was electrified with excitement over a variety of formulations of eugenics theory. The grand optimism of the eugenics enterprise is evident in another passage from Galton:

> What Nature does blindly, slowly, and ruthlessly, man may do providently, quickly, and kindly. As it lies within his power, so it becomes his duty to work in that direction; just as it is his duty to succour neighbours who suffer misfortune. The improvement of our stock seems to me one of the highest objects that we can reasonably attempt.[39]

It should be noted that the spirit of Galton's description is both optimistic and compassionate. Eugenics, he suggests, offers a realistic hope that at last the human race has the capacity to manage its own destiny. The perennial problems of human society to which earlier generations had simply to resign themselves can be addressed scientifically— and through a scientific approach they can be *eliminated.* Depressing and expensive remedies such as prisons, poor-houses, insane asylums may still be necessary, but they will be far rarer than they are at present. The great hope of eugenics is that the quality of human life can be enhanced through more than an improvement of social institutions; the hope of eugenics is that the quality of human life can be enhanced through an improvement of the *human species* itself. This spirit of optimism is evident in what Marie Stopes' said in an address she gave at Queens Hall in London on May 30, 1921:

> The evolution of mankind in the past has been blind and blundering; our race has been recruited by accident, by chance, by misery, by crime; but from today we who are here may go forth as missionaries... who will make a feasible and possible thing, this great era of humanity. . . [when men and women] will bring forth an entirely new type of human creature, stepping into a future so beautiful, so full of the real joy of self-expression and understanding that we here today may look upon our grandchildren and think only that the gods have descended to walk upon the earth.[40]

Although she shared Galton's optimism— and the general optimism about eugenics that prevailed at the time— it was something other than high spirits that brought Marie Stopes and other feminists of the period to embrace the doctrine. Instead, they were prompted to advocate for eugenics as an extension of their feminist agenda. If women were to gain equal rights— in particular, if they were to assert control over their reproductive lives and thereby gain a *realistic* opportunity to become educated and to develop professional careers— then an awareness of the demographic consequences of that great transition must be faced squarely and honestly. These demographic consequences did not require advanced mathematical skills to appreciate. In *Wise Parenthood*, Stopes describes what she sees as the impending crisis in words calculated to evoke a sense of alarm:

. . . the numbers of our population increasingly tend to be made up from the less thrifty and the less conscientious. Were this only a superficial matter, it would concern the race but little, but it is penetratingly profound and far-reaching. The thriftless who breed so rapidly tend by that very fact to bring forth children who are weakened and handicapped by physical as well as mental warping and weakness, and at the same time to demand their support from the sound and thrifty. It is indeed most serious for any race when . . . less than half the population is "physically fit," even when fitness is judged by the comparatively low standard of present-day needs. *Wise Parenthood,* p. 47

Ironically, the success of feminism might be said to abet this disturbing demographic trend. The feminist agenda marched forward on the birth control policies so vigorously advocated by Stopes and others. But if the most talented women in society, those who were best able to take advantage of the education indispensible to professional advancement, radically curtailed their reproduction, the result would be— less talented children. And by contrast, so went the concern, the less talented women in society, those least able to benefit from education, would reproduce disproportionately. The distressing conclusion seemed to be that what is good for women is bad for society.

For early 20th century feminists, the way around this apparent impasse was eugenics. It was their idealism and their belief in social progress that made a commitment to eugenics inevitable. In their view, feminism without eugenics would precipitate a genetic disaster. Without eugenics, the feminist agenda would be nothing more than a selfish assertion of privilege by educated women who were already privileged. While we in the 21st century might not approve of the specifics of their plans to implement eugenics, the feminists of a century ago were dedicated to social responsibility. They saw their struggle for women's rights in a broader context of the betterment of society and the species. And to say it again, they took eugenics to be necessary precisely *because* they took the implementation of feminism to be a social and moral imperative. Without a eugenic dimension to feminism, the result of any success of the feminist movement would be a weakening both of society and the human species. As with her advocacy of birth control, Stopes is impatient with the congenial middle and upper class mentality that arranges, for reasons of psychological convenience, to not think about the implicit *realities* of the circumstances evident in the streets of daily urban life. Speaking of the fictitious "Mrs. Jones" in her article in the *London Daily Mail,* Marie forcefully makes the point:

> The serious truth is that not many of the leisured and learned have bothered to think out the meaning of what she is doing. If they realized it, surely an outcry of dismay would be raised, *for Mrs. Jones is destroying the race!* "How Mrs. Jones Does Her Worst," p. 114

This concern about negative demographic consequences for the human race was not restricted to feminists. While he was president of the United States, Theodore Roosevelt raised the specter of "race suicide"— by which he meant the failure of Americans of Anglo-Saxon descent to reproduce themselves in sufficient numbers for the continuance of the racial subgroup. (Note that for Roosevelt, the word "race" means *Anglo-Saxon* race; by contrast, the word "race" in Stopes' writings typically means *human* race.) In a speech given to the National Congress of Mothers in 1905, President Roosevelt cautioned:

> No mother has an easy time, the most mothers have very hard times; and yet what true mother would barter her experience of joy and sorrow in exchange for a life of cold selfishness, which insists upon perpetual amusement and the avoidance of

care, and which often finds its fit dwelling place in some flat designed to furnish with the least possible expenditure of effort the maximum of comfort and of luxury, but in which there is literally no place for children?[41]

But the call to maternal responsibility issued by President Roosevelt (and others) sounded to many feminists all too much like a call back to the kitchen, to reproductive drudgery, and away from professional careers. Thank you, but no thank you. And yet the demographic consequences implicit in feminism could not be ignored.

Responding to this challenge, feminists of a century ago devised an alternative strategy. Rather than promoting the reproductive *increase* of talented women, many advocated the reproductive *decrease* of the less talented. This strategy found strident voice both in Europe and in America. It was often suggested that a walk through any city would make the core of the demographic problem evident. Typical were these observations by Stopes in her essay "The Control of Parenthood: Imperial and Racial Aspects":

> The race pictured in the Utopias— the human race as it may be— must have not only well-developed and sufficiently beautiful and adaptable bodies, it must have minds increasingly attuned to the ideal . . . But a deep underlying truth is the fact that the expression of the potentialities of a mind depend on the bodily form through which they act, as does the electric current depend on the wires of the lamp for its transmutation into light. What of the minds that are formed in the crowded spaces of an overburdened mother? Can they be well formed in the poison of bitterness provoked by the anguish and horror of undesired maternity? "Control of Parenthood," p. 109

There was a problem, however, one that was recognized at once: the less talented were not likely to acknowledge the need for restricting their numbers. No matter that such policies could be argued to improve their own lives, the drive to reproduce is one of the most primordial imperatives installed in animal life— including human life— through the processes of evolution. In the face of this genetically based ground of resistance, *compulsory sterilization* was a policy that recommended itself to those feminists who took seriously the threat of a demographic crisis.

It is an unpleasant fact that most prominent feminists of the early 20th century— not only Stopes, but also Margaret Sanger and others in the United States— advocated the legislation of policies that are, in light of today's values, abhorrent. They believed they could correct for the negative demographic consequences of feminism through coercive programs that rode roughshod over the rights and dignity of individual women who were judged to be *sub-standard*. They believed that eugenic ends justified means that we today would pronounce criminal.

To understand— not to *justify,* but to understand— how feminists and other social idealists, people such as Stopes and Sanger, could embrace such expedients, it is necessary to consider them in terms of the consciousness of their own times, rather than simply condemn them in terms of the values of the 21st century. We must keep in mind, in our analyses, that we know things that they did not, could not, know. If we are to understand Marie Stopes' ideas on eugenics, and the urgency with which she presented them, we must resolve to give attention to the sense of *crisis* that haunted the thinking of her time about feminism and demography. To state it simply— and perhaps over-simply— we today assess the eugenic programs of the early 20th century through the lens of *human rights.* But those who advocated those programs were thinking more in terms of *public health.* And a public health agenda is one that has historically been allowed a higher degree of *invasiveness* than, say, a criminal justice agenda. For example, the rules of engagement against an epidemic of *influenza* will often allow more intrusion into individual liberties than will a so-called "crime epidemic." Put otherwise, in a public health crisis, the balance between individual rights and community welfare tips to favor community welfare.

The crisis at issue, Stopes urged her readers to see, was a public health issue so acute as to justify invasive procedures. And she did not shrink from the implications of this assessment: she took the impending crisis to warrant Draconian measures. And she called into question whether there is a universal right to exercise one of the most primordial of human motives, the urge to reproduce:

> The power of parenthood ought no longer to be exercised by all, however inferior, as an "individual right." It is profoundly a duty and a privilege, and it is essentially the concern of the whole community. It should be the policy of the community to encourage in every way the parenthood of those whose circumstances and conditions are such that there is a reasonable anticipation that they will give rise to healthy, well-endowed future citizens. It should be the policy of the community to discourage from parenthood all whose circumstances are such as would make probable the introduction of weakened, diseased or debased future citizens. *Radiant Motherhood*, p. 77-78

It is true that demographic concerns are the legitimate concerns of the community, but while Stopes uses the terms "encourage" and "discourage," she clearly has something more forceful in mind. A few pages further in *Radiant Motherhood*, she speaks of "the terrible debasing power of the inferior, the depraved and feeble-minded . . . this prolific depravity must be curbed. How shall this be done? A very few quite simple Acts of Parliament could deal with it." (p. 83) And what *kind* of "simple Acts of Parliament" were needed? We read next of her proposals for state-mandated sterilization, for both men and women. For men, sterilization could be accomplished through vasectomy. This was deemed to be a far more humane procedure than castration: "To castrate any male is, of course, not only to deprive him of his manhood and thus to injure his personal consciousness, but to remove bodily organs, the loss of which adversely affects his mentality. . ." (p. 84) And for women, "X-ray" sterilization, although it induces shudders in the 21st century mind, was deemed to be a more humane procedure than tubal ligation— salpingectomy, as it was then called. To many, the fact that such procedures were performed under the banner of "humane treatment" only adds to the sinister overtones of the programs. Connecting her proposals to the optimistic visions of eugenics that prevailed in her day, Stopes assures her readers that such fine aspirations can be realized only through the legislation of involuntary sterilization of the less-than-fit:

> When Bills are passed to ensure the sterility of the hopelessly rotten and racially diseased, and to provide for the education of the childbearing woman so that she spaces her children healthily, our race will rapidly quell the stream of depraved, hopeless and wretched lives which are at present ever increasing in proportion in our midst. Before this stream at present the thoughtful shrink but do nothing. Such action as will be possible when these bills are passed will . . . increase the relative *proportion* of the sound and healthy among us who may consciously contribute to the higher and more beautiful forms of the human race. . . *Radiant Motherhood,* p. 85-86

And in many countries throughout the world, such bills were passed. In the early decades of the 20th century, many European nations passed legislation for the sterilization of the mentally unfit; Germany under National Socialism is only the most notorious example. Notably, such laws did not become legislated in Great Britain. Equally notable, such legislation was enacted with enthusiasm by many states in the United States— including Indiana, Washington, California, and Virginia. The latter, Virginia, is a case that is particularly relevant historically. The state of Virginia passed a law in 1924 allowing sterilization of the mentally retarded. A sterilization program was operated by the state at the Lynchburg Colony for the Epileptic and Feebleminded, where beginning in 1927, until its termination in 1974 (yes, 1974), children considered to be sub-par, or "feebleminded," were forcibly sterilized. Consent forms were signed, but reportedly under conditions of coercion and confusion. A young woman, Carrie Buck, was scheduled for sterilization on grounds of feeblemindedness. The decision was appealed, and the case found its way to the Supreme Court in 1927, where it was decided in favor of the state of Virginia (represented by Lynchburg Colony administrator Dr. James H. Bell). Carrie Buck was sterilized. But the Supreme Court case Buck v. Bell has become infamous— cited by opponents of eugenics as emblematic of the agenda of any project for human enhancement. Subsequent investigation into the case has suggested that Carrie Buck was not, in fact, "feebleminded." She was poor, came from a family that was seen as disreputable, and had become pregnant by being raped by her step-mother's nephew. Being from the "wrong" stock, being unmarried and pregnant— these are what brought about her incarceration at the Lynchburg Colony. No matter that it was an outrage of justice, in the spirit of the times Carrie Buck's treatment was taken to serve public welfare. The Supreme Court decision was written by one of the most eminent of American legal and philosophical thinkers, Oliver Wendell Holmes. His words have been cited in almost every hostile study of eugenics, and merit repetition here. Concurring with Dr. Bell's claim that Carrie Buck "is the probable potential parent of socially inadequate offspring, likewise afflicted, that she may be sexually sterilized without detriment to her general health and that her welfare and that of society will be promoted by her sterilization," Holmes concludes:

> We have seen more than once that the public welfare may call upon the best citizens for their lives. It would be strange if it could not call upon those who already sap the strength of the State for these lesser sacrifices . . . in order to prevent our being swamped with incompetence. It is better for all the world, if instead of waiting to execute degenerate offspring for crime, or to let them starve for their imbecility, society can prevent those who are manifestly unfit from continuing their kind . . . Three generations of imbeciles are enough.[42]

Alas, the reputation of a fine thinker stands compromised and stained by these words. It will not do to blink at the outrageous intrusiveness of the sterilization policies proposed by Stopes and put into the force of law by jurists like Holmes. Nor must we allow ourselves to be unaware of the fact that such recommendations as those of Marie Stopes and legal precedents such as those of Oliver Wendell Holmes were eagerly seized upon by Nazi ideologues who used them as models for policies vastly more deadly than the forced sterilization programs in America. What are we to conclude? Were the advocates of eugenics of a century ago, feminists like Maries Stopes among them, ethical monsters? Were they, as some today insist, harbingers of the dark intentions that were to be institutionalized as National Socialism? Our approach to such questions is, of course, powerfully colored by our historical awareness of the horrific extremes to which such enthusiasms can lead. For many people today, eugenics is a byword for gross injustice, even for mass murder. And alas, there are plausible reasons for this assessment. This explains why eugenics is a *notorious* idea rather than an *interesting* one.

Before proceeding, there is a question that calls to be addressed: If the word eugenics is so loaded with negative historical freight, why not choose another word? In fact, there are alternatives— for example "transhumanism" and "human enhancement." Nicolas Agar, in his 2004 study titled *Liberal Eugenics: In Defence of Human Enhancement,* claims that there are two reasons why the word *eugenics* should be used— and his reasons are good ones. First, if we are to speak of and endorse proposals that are indisputably eugenic, yet decline to call them by their familiar name, it "smacks of Orwellian redefinition." To avoid the word "eugenics" seems like *avoidance* in the pejorative sense; to avoid the controversial word is to lack directness and candor, it conveys a sense of evasiveness. A refusal to clearly *own* the word historically associated with eugenic theory seems an oblique acknowledgement that one takes oneself to be trafficking in dishonorable intentions. A second and more important point made by Agar is this: "Anyone advocating such a programme must demonstrate an awareness of the errors of the past."[43]

Talk of eugenics in the 21st century must keep ever in mind the misdirected eugenic policies implemented in the 20th century. Any serious discussion of eugenics today must forcefully assert how a social implementation of eugenic ideals will *not* entail a replay of social policies of the early 20th century (and I do not refer here only to Nazism, but also to policies implemented in the Unites States) that seem so grotesque and embarrassing— not to mention criminal— in the 21st century.

How are we to assess those intellectuals of the early decades of the 20th century who so heartily endorsed eugenics? To review, they include not only the usual suspects like Herbert Spencer, Charles Darwin, and Francis Galton, but also figures like George Bernard Shaw, H. G. Wells, Theodore Roosevelt, Margaret Sanger, W. E. B.

DuBois, Edward Bellamy, Oliver Wendell Holmes. And of course, there were lesser known lights like Marie Stopes, Charlotte Perkins Gilman, and Frances Swiney. Were all these individuals simply racists? By today's standards, some were. But to fairly assess them in the 21st century, we must situate their thinking in the context both of what they believed they knew, and of what they did not know.

What they believed they knew was that applied genetics, eugenics, might mitigate human misery to a historically unprecedented degree. What they believed they knew was that eugenics might make possible the implementation of a *socially responsible* feminist agenda.

What they did not know was the extent that eugenics theory could be pressed into service not of enlightened and humanistic ideals, but into the service of atavistic and tribalist agendas of hate and insecurity. What they did not know is what we of the 21st century know all too well: the despicable things that could be done in the name of eugenics through an ideology like that of National Socialism.

And this brings us back to Marie Stopes. For reasons that we've seen are understandable, many people take the word "eugenics" to evoke Nazi atrocities— atrocities that are assumed to have *something* to do with eugenics. Consider the opening words of a recent well-received book on eugenics by Elof Axel Carlson, titled *The Unfit: A History of a Bad Idea.* Carlson states the agenda of his study:

> *The Unfit: A History of a Bad Idea* explores the sources of a movement that was used to justify, at least among those who had the authority to implement it, the final solution or Holocaust, which claimed several millions of innocent lives in World War II. The movement is usually called eugenics. . .[44]

In the 21st century there is broad agreement with Carlson's assertion that the Holocaust was nothing more or less than applied eugenics. This assumption is sustained by some of what Marie Stopes put into her writings. A typical example is the following passage from *Wise Parenthood*. It is clear that Stopes intended to issue a call to common sense. But in a world that has experienced the Nazi era, her words have a sinister ring:

> Whatever theory of the transmission of characteristics scientists may ultimately adopt, there can be little doubt in the minds of rational people that heredity *does* tell, and that children who descend from a double line of healthy and intelligent parents are better equipped to face whatever difficulties in their environment may later arise than are children from unsound stock. As Sir James Barr said in the *British Medical journal,* 1918: "There is no equality in nature among children nor among adults, and if there is to be a much-needed improvement in the race, we must breed from the physically, morally and intellectually fit." *Wise Parenthood,* p. 34

This passage is especially relevant to our discussion because it is quoted in a BBC documentary titled *The Occult History of the Third Reich,* in an episode titled "The SS: Blood and Soil." Marie Stopes is prominently named, and pages of *Wise Parenthood* are displayed. The narrator, in a voice drenched in shocked disbelief, relates that Stopes' book is dedicated "To all those who wish to see our race thrive." Stopes is placed among what is presented as a cabal of twisted intellectuals who provided the theoretical justification for the horrors of Nazi regime.

In another association of Marie Stopes with Nazi ideology, we hear an Australian member of parliament, one J. F. Coates, declare in 1940, the dark early days of World War II, that "The Empire today has three enemies— all from Munich. One is Hitler, the other Goebbels, and the other is that doctor of German philosophy and science— Dr Marie Stopes. The greatest of these is Marie Stopes."[45]

Because it is associated with racism, and even with genocide, eugenics is for many well-intentioned people not a candidate for rational assessment, but only for righteous condemnation. This is typically so, to say it again, in the intellectual world of the 21st century.

But there are, and there always have been, very different ways of relating to the enterprise called eugenics. We return to ancient Greece, but this time to a period long before Plato lived. Dating from the 8th century B.C.E., Homer's epic *The Iliad* offers what I suggest is a useful cue for thinking about eugenics in the 21st century. The Trojan hero Hektor, returning in full armor from the day's battle, reaches out for his infant son. The baby squeaks with fright, not recognizing Dad in his horse-hair helmet. Hektor removes the helmet, his infant son recognizes him and dives into his arms— all recognizably and touchingly *human*. Then Hektor holds the child over his head, and offers the following prayer:

> "Zeus, and you other immortals, grant that this boy, who is my son, may be as I am, pre-eminent among the Trojans, great in strength, as am I, and rule strongly over Ilion; and some day let them say of him 'He is better by far than his father'."[46]

Hektor's prayer speaks the aspiration of eugenics. It gives eloquent voice to a hope that is entirely human, one that any parent will recognize. He prayed that his son would be "better by far than his father." This is a prayer rooted in love, not in sinister intention. For Hektor, the details of his son's surpassing him would center on the qualities that Hektor and his culture prized— that the boy would become a strong warrior and a brilliant leader. While the specifics Hektor had in mind might vary from 21st century hopes, the general aspiration is a recognizable one. Like Hektor, we want our offspring to be not merely healthy, but *healthier*. We want them to be not just smart, but, if possible, *smarter*. We want them not just to have admirable character; we want them to be *more* admirable. This model of eugenics is one of the most intimate of human aspirations, one that developed over thousands and thousands of generations of human and pre-human evolution. It is woven into our genes, it is part of the human heritage. To attempt to deny it is to attempt to deny ourselves. And this aspiration is given voice by Marie Stopes, when she says:

> It is my prayer that I may present such a racial ideal, not only to my own people but to humanity. It is my prayer that I may live to see in the generation of my grandchildren a humanity from which almost all the most blackening and distressing elements have been eliminated, and in which the vernal bodily beauty and unsullied spiritual power of those then growing up will surpass anything that we know to-day except among the rare and gifted few. This is not a wild dream; it is a real potentiality almost within reach. *Radiant Motherhood,* p. 81

Eugenics, as Marie Stopes understands it, is an extension of mother-love. The concerns of eugenics begin with one's own children, extends to grandchildren— and beyond. It is noteworthy that she claims concern "not only to my own people but to *humanity.*" This indicates a fundamental incompatibility of Stopes' vision of eugenics with that of National Socialist ideology. In the latter, eugenic concern was restricted to what is in fact an illusory construct— the Aryan people, understood to be genetically distinct from other human population groups.

But as I emphasized earlier, the fact that Marie Stopes was not an ideological fellow-traveler with Nazis does mean that her ideas merit breezy acceptance. Proposals were put forward that we would today find appalling in their class and racial biases— put forward not just by Marie Stopes, but by the many prominent intellectuals who publically speculated on the issue. It was a different world, a world largely *innocent* of the extremes to which such proposals could lead.

Today, the closing words in Stopes' essay "The Control of Parenthood" convey to the 21st century reader a sense of chill rather than optimism:

> The first foundation of Utopia, could be reached in my lifetime, had I the power to issue inviolable edicts. Alas I, that the age of a beneficent autocracy has never been and is not here to-day! Instead of achieving in two generations the great result on the human race that could be materialised, it will be necessary to take the slower means of creating in every individual that intense consciousness of the race which will make it impossible for individuals ever to tolerate the coercion of enforced and miserable motherhood, with its consequent poison of the racial stream. "The Control of Parenthood" p. 112

Marie's words convey a chill of foreboding not just because of what we know of the history of National Socialism. "Beneficent autocracy" has all too often been the self-assurance of those who have wrought disaster on humanity— Hitler is only one on a list of those who would improve the human prospect through beneficent autocracy. As we have already seen in discussing *Radiant Motherhood,* the agenda supported by Stopes was involuntary sterilization imposed on those deemed unfit. It is worth revisiting the passage. Prefacing her strategies for a "humane" implementation of coercive sterilization, she says this:

> . . . if the good in our race is not to be swamped and destroyed by the debased as the fine tree by the parasite, this prolific depravity must be curbed. How shall this be done? A very few quite simple Acts of Parliament could deal with it. *Radiant Motherhood,* p. 83

It bears repetition that Stopes and other early advocates of eugenics lived in a different world— "another country," where they do things differently, as L. P. Hartley put it. But the difference between the world a century ago and our world today is not that they practiced eugenics and we do not. Quite the contrary, eugenics is practiced apace in today's world— at least by those able to do so. It is practiced under the relatively respectable guise of genetic counseling, and in the emergence of sperm banks for artificial insemination applicants. The difference between our world and the world of a century ago is that they could *talk* about eugenics, and we cannot. In the world addressed by Marie Stopes, the perceived demographic crisis could be addressed out loud, publically and with candor. Then, talk about the health and quality of populations was not taken to be disreputable. Today, by contrast, talk of the improvement of populations, of the human species itself, takes place, if at all, *sotto voce.* And there are good reasons for that. To speak favorably of eugenics is to take a stroll on thin ice: it is to put your reputation and your career at risk. This, despite the fact— and this is the interesting point of the story— this despite the fact that the *practice* of eugenics is becoming increasingly commonplace.

This cannot be overemphasized: although it is taboo to *talk* about eugenics, except to condemn it, it is at the same time increasingly fashionable to *practice* eugenics. How is this possible? Consider some examples. In the May 2, 2003, issue of *The Chronicle of Higher Education,* a story from the island of Cyprus is reported. In the article, pointedly titled "Choosing Eugenics," Lila Guterman writes that—

> Both the Greek and Turkish sides of the divided island have instituted mandatory programs to eliminate thalassemia, a horrific inherited blood disease. In both regions, before getting married, people must get tested to find out if they have the gene that causes thalassemia. From that point on, people can make their own decisions. If carriers of the gene decide to marry and have children anyway, the women can then voluntarily undergo prenatal testing to see if their fetus is

doomed to the disease. And in both regions, if parents choose to end a pregnancy, the state will pay for the abortion.[47]

In America, the social critic Walter Truett Anderson relates a similar development in New York City:

> In 1993 *The New York Times* ran a story, rich with historical irony, about a community of Orthodox Jews who have a program of genetic testing for young people. The goal of the program is simple: to eliminate common inherited diseases such as Tay-Sachs and cystic fibrosis. Among Ashkenazi Jews, one person in twenty-five is a carrier of the Tay-Sachs gene, and one person in twenty-five is a carrier of cystic fibrosis.[48]

The elimination of undesirable traits like genetic diseases is, in the established discourse about eugenics, called *negative* eugenics. The orientation is preventative, and the policies are typically scripted as part of a public health agenda. But it cannot be denied that the practice *is* eugenics. Anderson continues his narrative:

> . . . every year, representatives of the Committee for Prevention of Jewish Genetic Diseases go to the Orthodox high schools and offer the students a blood test. Those tested are given an identification number . . . When a boy and a girl are being considered by the community's matchmakers as likely prospects to be united in marriage, the next step is to call the office hotline for their identification numbers . . . The ancient Jewish tradition of matchmaking, in short, has moved into the bio-information age.[49]

The project was named *Dor Yeshorim,* or "generation of the righteous." Its success rate, Anderson reports, was impressive: the dreaded Tay-Sachs disease has been eliminated from the community. A splendid success, but as Anderson points out, "by any name, it is eugenics." And, he continues, as with this community of Orthodox Jews, so it will be with the rest of society: "Eugenics is part of life in our time, and the challenge is to understand that and manage it wisely." Fully aware of the dark historical baggage that attends the enterprise, Anderson takes his stand on the *aspirations* of eugenics, not on its hateful miscarriages. He concludes his discussion— "If this be eugenics, let us make the most of it."

The negative eugenics spoken of by Anderson, with its focus on the elimination of undesirable traits, is not the only form of eugenics practiced commonly in today's society. The popular television news program "60 Minutes," broadcast on March 19, 2006, presented a report on the success of artificial insemination in America. According to correspondent Steve Kroft, 30,000 children are born each year to women inseminated by anonymous sperm donors. That of itself is interesting, but even more interesting for our purposes is a donor known by the code designed to protect his privacy— 48QAH.[50]

Through an online database, a group of mothers who had been artificially inseminated— many with conspicuously gifted children— discovered that the donor by whom they'd conceived their children was 48QAH. And, it turned out, this donor was willing to make his identity known. He is Matthew Niedner, a pediatrician. While in medical school, Niedner was a frequent sperm donor, and it is estimated that his donations may have yielded more than a hundred children. A hundred *talented* children. Nothing was said of it in the program, but it cannot be denied that the "contributions" of Dr. Niedner are *eugenic* in their effect.

The augmentation of desirable traits, traits like physical health, intelligence, and self-discipline, is called *positive* eugenics. In the catalogs through which prospective mothers "shop" for sperm donors, never, but never, does one find on offer educational dropouts, dayworkers, or layabouts. In his readable book *The Genius Factory,* David Plotz presents a typical sample from the 1985 edition of the Repository for Germinal Choice catalog. Donor #36 is attractively presented as "A professional man of very high standing in his field; has had a book published, excels in mathematics." But there's more: not only is #36 "very good looking," he also has hobbies— "writing, reading, chess and piano." And in the bargain, he "excels in many sports."[51]

Such policies are clearly benign, and they are so because they lack a crucial element of earlier proposals for eugenics— emphatically including those of Marie Stopes. That crucial element is *coercion.* Blithe assurances by Stopes that "a very few quite simple Acts of Parliament could deal with it" strike us, rightly, as outrageous. Appropriately so. But more appropriate, more urgent, is that we can *learn* from the missteps of Stopes and so many others. And the one thing to be learned is that coercion is *never* justified. Put otherwise, the ends, however noble they may be thought to be, do not justify the means. Means are justified— or not— solely on their own terms. Any other approach opens the door to institutionalized injustice through corrupt public policies employed— for the best and highest motives. Breezy references to omelets and broken eggs are callous evasions, and are dishonorable. That is what we stand to learn from earlier hopes to implement eugenic aspirations.

In the near future, we will come to talk about the eugenic strategies that, as described above, are already in practice. No doubt the discussions of policy specifics will be contentious. That's as it should be— a sign of a healthy society. As a culture, we will in the near future publically think and rethink policies like those of the *Dor Yeshorim* program in New York and the various enterprises implementing artificial insemination. And others. Yes, there will be those who insist that plans to implement any euthanasia strategies are criminal in their intent. But increasingly, such strident indictments will be taken to be in the same category as the "abortion is murder" enthusiasts who rowdy that debate with moral invective.

6

The Daughter of Time Clears Her Throat

Marie Stopes was an activist, and typically, the activist mentality is not one much given to doubts and second thoughts. She was a person who thrived on adversity, and relished being controversial. In this, many of her friends warned her throughout her life, she was her own worst enemy.

Everything we know about Marie Stopes— whether through her own writings or through the various biographical studies on her— suggests that she was a highly complex and interesting person, an intense and forceful person. At the same time, however, what we read both by and about her suggests that Marie Stopes was not an especially *appealing* person.

We have a habit of scanning history and finding "good guys" and "bad guys." For that reason, Marie Stopes is not an easy figure to understand. Complexity, inconsistency, even incoherence were essential aspects of her highly idiosyncratic personality. No doubt that's the case for many people. But with Stopes these characteristics incorporated extremes that served to make her— extraordinary. We find a wonderful intelligence and an iron determination; she is audacious; she is often arrogant and imperious. She speaks of ideals that are aspirational; she gives voice to a mystical eroticism. She is at one and the same time an iconoclast and a dogmatist. In addition, there is often a disturbingly totalitarian edge to her recommendations— a predictable by-product, perhaps, of the social activist who would save society and feels impeded by the dullards who comprise society, dullards who don't really give a damn about being saved. Marie Stopes is, in the rear-view mirror of history, easy to admire, and equally easy to despise. A 21st century assessment of her work and character depends powerfully on the eyes of the person looking into that historical mirror.

In her day, many people were shocked by both her sexually explicit language and (even worse) by her claim that the healthy woman will enjoy a vigorous sexual life, attended by vigorous sexual appetites. This was more than a revolution in employment policies— more even than a revolution in morality. Here was a revolution that shook the foundations of the human project, a revolution that shook the foundations of religion, morality, politics, and education. And decent people were shocked.

But the Daughter of Time changed her tune. No matter if her name is not widely known, today Stopes' views on sexuality, and also her concerns on the importance of disseminating those views to all segments of the population, is commonplace. Such attitudes are taken to be indispensable not only to an authentic feminism, but to a general psychological health among humans. Evidence of this is found in the easy availability of books like Sari Locker's *The Complete Idiot's Guide to Amazing Sex*.

In her day, enthusiasm and forceful advocacy of eugenics were commonplace, especially among intellectuals, both conservative and liberal, and even more particularly among feminists. Eugenics was promoted not only by scientists and social theorists, but also by progressive religious leaders. A century ago, such advocacy was not seen as shocking, but rather as common sense.

But the Daughter of Time has again changed her tune. Today it is commonplace to take *any* talk about eugenics that is not unqualified condemnation to be a species of hate speech. The agenda of eugenics is, in the 21st century, handcuffed to one of the ugliest episodes in history— Nazism. And any who advocate it today are judged to be guilty by association. Just that was the case in the BBC documentary *The Occult History of the Third Reich,* referred to above, in which Marie Stopes was retroactively indicted as a co-conspirator with the Nazis. Decent people are shocked.

And now, the Daughter of Time is again clearing her throat; once again, the truth she speaks discloses her parentage. Once again, our understanding of what we take to be "the truth" is changing. And for the best of reasons. History shows unambiguously that there are practices and principles that are preferable— the social habits that confer survival advantages for those who adhere to them. In his 2004 book, *The Empty Cradle,* demographer Phillip Longman assesses developments in the populations of the industrialized world of the late 20th and early 21st centuries. He observes:

> We are headed toward a future in which only rich people will be able to afford to raise and educate a child, and rich people, generally, are not much interested in the work. If they were, they would not be rich. . . An economy that creates disincentives to have children, while under-compensating parents and other caregivers for the essential human capital they create, is living beyond its means.[52]

What Longman expresses is the very concern faced by feminists a century ago— the demographic consequences of the *success* of a feminist agenda that is rooted, as it must be, in birth control. Industrialized societies, in which women are increasingly educated and empowered, are clearly at risk. The most dramatic example is Japan, where birthrates have declined sharply since World War II, and which is regularly described by contemporary demographers as an emergent geriatric nation. What have been earnestly guarded as personal and private choices, reproductive choices, are once again being considered in light of their social impacts. The specter of what Theodore Roosevelt decried as "race suicide" is once again abroad in the world— not, this time, with a focus on the Anglo-Saxon race, but on national economies and social stability. Longman dares to suggest that it is time to rethink the status of reproductive choices as being sacrosanct and immune from critique. Speaking of the prevailing view of childlessness as merely a matter of lifestyle choice, he says:

> . . . this view is that people who decide not to have children hurt no one, or even benefit society, and so cannot be criticized . . . The problem with these attitudes is that they fail to account for the deepening dependency all people have on both the quantity and quality of other people's children.[53]

For most people, the impending demographic crisis spoken of by Longman is a mere dot on the horizon. But this cannot last much longer; when the dot becomes a thunder cloud, we will, as a culture, be brought to not only practice eugenics— after the fashion of the *Dor Yeshorim* program and artificial insemination clinics discussed above— but also to *talk* about eugenics. We will do this not because we want to, but because we will feel a *need* to. And we will feel that need for the same reasons that feminists and progressives felt it eighty years ago: the demographic consequences of the *success* of the feminist agenda are asserting themselves throughout the world. To cite Longman again, "If no alternative solution can be found, the future will belong to those who reject markets, reject learning, reject modernity, and reject freedom. This will be the fundamentalist movement." This is why we will begin to *talk* about eugenics in addition to practicing it. This, at least in part, is why the Daughter of Time is once again about to change her tune.

ENDNOTES

1   Rose, J. *Marie Stopes and the Sexual Revolution.*
    London: Faber and Faber, 1993, p. 65.

2   Rose, *Marie Stopes and the Sexual Revolution,* p. 78.

3   Hall, R. *Passionate Crusader: the Life of Marie Stopes.*
    New York: Harcourt Brace Jovanovich, 1977, p. 251.

4   *New Witness,* September 12, 1919. Cited in Hall, R.
    Passionate Crusader: the Life of Marie Stopes. New
    York: Harcourt Brace Jovanovich, 1977, p. 150.

5   Sutherland, H. G. *Birth Control: a Statement of
    Christian Doctrine against the Neo-Malthusians.* Project
    Gutenberg: http://www.gutenberg. org/dirs/etext05/8bctr
    10.txt. 1922, Chapter VII, section 6.b.

6   Hall, R., ed. *Dear Dr. Stopes: Sex in the 1920's.*
    London: Andre Deutsch, 1978, p. 205.

7   Hall, *Passionate Crusader: the Life of Marie Stopes,* p.
    259.

8   Hall, *Passionate Crusader,* p. 260.

9   Hall, *Passionate Crusader,* p. 325.

10   Maude, A. *Marie Stopes: Her Work and Play.* New York: G. P. Putnam's Sons, 1933, p. 40.

11   Cited in Maude, *Marie Stopes: Her Work and Play,* p. 149-150.

12   The Lambeth Conference Archives, 6th Conference, 1920. http://www. lambethconference.org/resolutions/ 1920/

13   Hall, *Dear Dr. Stopes,* p. 68.

14   Pagels, E. *Adam, Eve, and the Serpent.* New York: Vintage Books, 1989,   p. 29.

15   Sanger, M. *Woman and the New Race,* Chapter XIII. Battalions of Unwanted Babies the Cause of War. http://www.bartleby.com/1013/ 13.html.

16   Locker, S. *The Complete Idiot's Guide to Amazing Sex.* New York: Alpha Books, 2005, p. 165.

17   Hall, *Passionate Crusader,* p. 19.

18   Wilder, T. *Our Town.* New York: Avon Books, 1976, p. 99.

19   Hall, *Passionate Crusader,* p. 112.

20   Hall, *Passionate Crusader,* p. 128.

21   Maude, A. *Marie Stopes: Her Work and Play,* p. 138.

22 Rose, *Marie Stopes and the Sexual Revolution,* p. 111.

23 Gilman, C. P. *The Living of Charlotte Perkins Gilman.* New York: Harper Colophon Books, 1963, p. 323.

24 Gilman, *The Living of Charlotte Perkins Gilman,* p. 327.

25 Robb, G. "Between Science and Spiritualism: Frances Swiney's Vision of a Sexless Future," in *Diogenes* 52:4, 2005, p. 166-7.

26 Gilman, C. P. *Herland.* New York: Dover Publications, 1998, p. 48-9.

27 For a fuller treatment of Ellis' views from the standpoint of today's feminist perspective, see Margaret Jackson's *The* Real *Facts of Life: Feminism and the Politics of Sexuality c 1850—1940.* London: Taylor & Francis, 1994, Chapter 5.

28 Ellis, H. *Studies in the Psychology of Sex, v.3, Part I,* "Love and Pain," section 1. Project Gutenberg: http://www.gutenberg.org/files/13612/ 13612-h/13612-h.htm#3_S_II.

29 Ellis, H. *Studies in the Psychology of Sex, v.5, Part II,* "The Mechanisms of Detumescence," section 3. Project Gutenberg: http://www.gutenberg.org/files/13614/13614-h/ 13614-h.htm#5_M_III.

30 Dijkstra, B. *Evil Sisters: the Threat of Female Sexuality and the Cult of Manhood.* New York: Alfred A. Knopf, 1996, pp.206-7.

31 Swiney, F. *The Bar of Isis: the Law of the Mother.* London: C. W. Daniel, 1909, pp. 24-5.

32 Robb G. "Between Science and Spiritualism: Frances Swiney's Vision of a Sexless Future," p. 165.

33 Blavatsky, H. P. *The Secret Doctrine, v.II.* Pasadena: Theosophical University Press, 1999, p. 411.

34 See *Wikipedia* article on "Comstock Law," http://en.wikipedia.org/wiki/ Comstock_Law.

35 Cited in Rose, *Marie Stopes and the Sexual Revolution,* p. 92.

36 Cited in Hall, *Passionate Crusader,* p. 321-322.

37 Darwin, C. *The Descent of Man (1871),* Ch.5, "Natural Selection as Affecting Civilized Nations." In *The Darwin Compendium.* New York: Barnes & Noble, 2005, p. 827.

38 Galton, F. *Inquiries into Human Faculty and Its Development,* 1883. Online edition: http://galton.org /books/human-faculty/text/ human-faculty.pdf#search= %22Galton%3A%20%22Inquiries%20into%20human% 20faculty%20and%20its%20development%22%22. Page17, fn 1.

39 Galton, F. *Essays in Eugenics, "Eugenics: Its Definition, Scope, and Aims."* Washington D.C.: Scott-Townsend Publishers, p. 42.

[40] Cited in Rose, *Marie Stopes and the Sexual Revolution,* p. 148-9.

[41] Roosevelt, T. "On American Motherhood." A speech given to the National Congress of Mothers, March 13, 1905. http://www.nationalcenter.org/TRooseveltMotherhood.html.

[42] Holmes, O. W. Decision in Buck v. Bell, 274 U.S. 200 (1927). http://www.law.du.edu/russell/lh/alh/docs/buckvbell.html.

[43] Agar, N. *Liberal Eugenics: In Defence of Human Enhancement.* Oxford: Blackwell Publishing, 2004, p. 5.

[44] Carlson, E. A. *The Unfit: A History of a Bad Idea.* Cold Spring Harbor, NY: Cold Spring Harbor Laboratory Press, 2001, p. 1.

[45] Hall, *Passionate Crusader,* epigraph.

[46] *The Iliad of Homer.* Translated by R. Lattimore. Chicago: University of Chicago Press, 1976. Book VI, lines 476-479.

[47] Guterman, L. "Choosing eugenics," in *The Chronicle of Higher Education.* 49:34, May 2, 2003, pp. A22-A26.

[48] Anderson, W. T. *Evolution Isn't What It Used To Be.* New York: W. H. Freeman and Company, 1996, p. 104.

[49] Anderson, *Evolution Isn't What It Used To Be,* p. 104.

50   The entire transcript of the "60 Minutes" segment, titled "Sperm Donor Siblings Find Family Ties," may be found at http://www.cbsnews.com/stories/2006/03/17/ 60minutes/printable1414965.shtml.

51   Plotz, D. *The Genius Factory: the Curious History of the Nobel Prize Sperm Bank.* New York: Random House, 2005, p. 182.

52   Longman, P. *The Empty Cradle: How Falling Birthrates Threaten World Prosperity.* New York: Basic Books, 2004, p. 145.

53   *Ibid.,* p. 138-140

Marie Stopes:

Essential Writings

Married Love (1918)

Author's Preface

MORE than ever to-day are happy homes needed. It is my hope that this book may serve the State by adding to their numbers. Its object is to increase the joys of marriage, and to show how much sorrow may be avoided.

The only secure basis for a present-day State is the welding of its units in marriage; but there is rottenness and danger at the foundations of the State if many of the marriages are unhappy. To-day, particularly in the middle classes in this country, marriage is far less really happy than its surface appears. Too many who marry expecting joy are bitterly disappointed; and the demand for 'freedom' grows; while those who cry aloud are generally unaware that it is more likely to have been their own ignorance than the 'marriage-bond' which was the origin of their unhappiness.

It is never *easy* to make marriage a lovely thing; and it is an achievement beyond the powers of the selfish, or the mentally cowardly. Knowledge is needed and, as things are at present, knowledge is almost unobtainable by those who are most in want of it.

The problems of the sex-life are infinitely complex, and for their solution urgently demand both sympathy and scientific research.

I have some things to say about sex, which, so far as I am aware, have not yet been said, things which seem to be of profound importance to men and women who hope to make their marriages beautiful.

This little book is less a record of a research than an attempt to present in easily understandable form the clarified and crystallised results of long and complex investigations. Its simple statements are based on a very large number of first-hand observations, on confidences from men and women of all classes and types, and on facts gleaned from wide reading . . .

I do not now touch upon the many human variations and abnormalities which bulk so largely in most books on sex, nor do I deal with the many problems raised by incurably unhappy marriages.

In the following pages I speak to those—and in spite of all our neurotic literature and plays they are in the great majority—who are nearly normal, and who are married or about to be married, and hope, but do not know how, to make their marriages beautiful and happy.

To the reticent, as to the conventional, it may seem a presumption or a superfluity to speak of the details of the most complex of all our functions. They ask: Is not instinct enough? The answer is No. Instinct is *not* enough. In every other human activity it has been realised that training, the handing on of tradition are essential. As Dr Saleeby once wisely pointed out: A cat knows how to manage her new-born kittens, how to bring them up and teach them; a human mother does not know how to manage her baby unless she is trained, either directly or by her own quick observation of other mothers. A cat performs her simple duties by instinct; a human mother has to be trained to fulfil her very complex ones.

The same is true in the subtle realm of sex. In this country, in modern times, the old traditions, the profound primitive knowledge of the needs of both sexes have been lost, and nothing but a muffled confusion of individual gossip disturbs a silence, shamefaced or foul. Here and there, in a family of fine tradition, a youth or maiden may learn some of the mysteries of marriage, but the great majority of people in our country have no glimmering of the supreme human art, the art of love; while in books on advanced Physiology and Medicine the gaps, the omissions, and even the misstatements of bare fact are amazing.

In my own marriage I paid such a terrible price for sex-ignorance that I feel that knowledge gained at such a cost should be placed at the service of humanity. In this little book average, healthy, mating creatures will find the key to the happiness which should be the portion of each. It has already guided some to happiness, and I hope it may save some others years of heartache and blind questioning in the dark.

CHAPTER I

The Heart's Desire

She gave him comprehension of the meaning of love: a word in many mouths, not often explained. With her, wound in his idea of her, he perceived it to signify a new start in our existence, a finer shoot of the tree stoutly planted in good gross earth; the senses running their live sap, and the minds companioned, and the spirits made one by the whole-natured conjunction. In sooth, a happy prospect for the sons and daughters of Earth, divinely indicating more than happiness: the speeding of us, compact of what we are, between the ascetic rocks and the sensual whirlpools, to the creation of certain nobler races, nor very dimly imagined. — GEORGE MEREDITH'S 'Diana of the Crossways,' chap. 37.

EVERY heart desires a mate. For some reason beyond our comprehension, nature has so created us that we are incomplete in ourselves; neither man nor woman singly can know the joy of the performance of all the human functions; neither man nor woman singly can create another human being. This fact, which is expressed in our outward divergencies of form, influences and colours the whole of our lives; and there is nothing for which the innermost spirit of one and all so yearns as for a sense of union with another soul, and the perfecting of oneself which such union brings.

In all young people, unless they have inherited depraved or diseased faculties, the old desire of our race springs up afresh in its pristine beauty.

With the dreams and bodily changes of adolescence, come to the youth and maiden the strange and powerful impulses of the racial instinct. The bodily differences of the two, now accentuated, become mystical, alluring, enchanting in their promise. Their differences unite and hold together the man and the woman so that their bodily union is the solid nucleus of an immense fabric of interwoven strands reaching to the uttermost ends of the earth; some lighter than the filmiest cobweb, or than the softest wave of music, iridescent with the colours, not only of the visible rainbow, but of all the invisible glories of the wave-lengths of the soul.

However much he may conceal it under assumed cynicism, worldliness, or self-seeking, the heart of every young man yearns with a great longing for the fulfilment of the beautiful dream of a lifelong union with a mate. Each heart knows instinctively that it is only a mate who can give full comprehension of all the potential greatness in the soul, and have tender laughter for all the child-like wonder that lingers so enchantingly even in the white-haired.

The search for a mate is a quest for an understanding heart clothed in a body beautiful, but unlike our own.

In the modern world, those who set out on high endeavours or who consciously separate themselves from the ordinary course of social life, are comparatively few, and it is not to them that I am speaking. The great majority of our citizens—both men and women—after a time of waiting, or of exploring, or of oscillating from one attraction to another, 'settle down' and marry.

Very few are actually so cynical as to marry without the hope of happiness; while most young people, however their words may deny it and however they may conceal their tender hopes by an assumption of cynicism, reveal that they are conscious of entering on a new and glorious state by their radiant looks and the joyous buoyancy of their actions. In the kisses and the hand touch of the betrothed are a zest and exhilaration which stir the blood like wine. The two read poetry, listen entranced to music which echoes the songs of their pulses, and see reflected in each other's eyes the beauty of the world. In the midst of this celestial intoxication they naturally assume that, as they are on the threshold of their lives, so too they are in but the ante-chamber of their experience of spiritual unity.

The more sensitive, the more romantic, and the more idealistic is the young person of either sex, the more his or her soul craves for some kindred soul with whom the whole being can unite. But all have some measure of this desire, even the most prosaic, and we know from innumerable stories of real life that the sternest man of affairs, he who may have worldly success of every sort, may yet, through the lack of a real mate, live with a sense almost as though the limbs of his soul had been amputated. Edward Carpenter has beautifully voiced this longing:—

That there should exist one other person in the world towards whom all openness of interchange should establish itself, from whom there should be no concealment; whose body should be as dear to one, in every part, as one's own; with whom there should be no sense of Mine or Thine, in property or possession; into whose mind one's thoughts should naturally flow, as it were to know themselves and to receive a new illumination; and between whom and oneself there should be a spontaneous rebound of sympathy in all the joys and sorrows and experiences of life; such is perhaps one of the dearest wishes of the soul.—'Love's Coming of Age.'

It may chance that someone into whose hands this book falls may protest that he or she has never felt the fundamental yearning to form a part of that trinity which alone is the perfect expression of humanity. If that is so, it is possible that all unconsciously he may be suffering from a real malady—sex anaesthesia. This is the name given to an inherent coldness, which, while it lacks the usual human impulse of tenderness, is generally quite unconscious of its lack. It may even be that the reader's departure from the ordinary ranks of mankind is still more fundamental, in which case, instead of sitting in judgment on the majority, he will do well to read some such book as 'The Sexual Question' (English translation 1908) by the famous Professor August Forel, in order that his own nature may be made known to him. He may then discover to which type of our widely various humanity he belongs. He need not read my book, for it is written about, and it is written for, ordinary men and women who, feeling themselves incomplete, yearn for a union that will have power not only to make a fuller and richer thing of their own lives, but which will place them in a position to use their sacred trust as creators of lives to come.

It has happened many times in human history that individuals have not only been able to conquer this natural craving for a mate, but have set up celibacy as a higher ideal. In its most beautiful expression and sublimest manifestations, the celibate ideal has proclaimed a world-wide love, in place of the narrower human love of home and children. Many saints and sages, reformers and dogmatists have modelled their lives on this ideal. But such individuals cannot be taken as the standard of the *race,* for they are out of its main current: they are branches which may flower, but never fruit in a bodily form.

In this world our spirits not only permeate matter but find their only expression through its medium. So long as we are human we must have bodies, and bodies obey chemical and physiological, as well as spiritual laws.

If our race as a whole set out to pursue an ideal which must ultimately eliminate bodies altogether, it is clear that very soon we should find the conditions of our environment so altered that we could no longer speak of the human race.

In the meantime, we *are* human. We each and all live our lives according to laws, some of which we have begun to understand, many of which are completely hidden from us. The most complete human being is he or she who consciously or unconsciously obeys the profound physical laws of our being in such a way that the spirit receives as much help and as little hindrance from the body as possible. A mind and spirit finds its fullest expression thwarted by the misuse, neglect or gross abuse of the body in which it dwells.

By the ignorant or self-indulgent breaking of fundamental laws endless harmonies are dislocated. The modern, small-minded ascetic endeavours to grow spiritually by destroying his physical instincts instead of by using them. But I would proclaim that we are set in the world so to mould matter that it may express our spirits; that it is presumption to profess to fight the immemorial laws of our physical being, and that he who does so loses unconsciously the finest flux in which wondrous new creations take their rise.

To use a homely simile—one might compare two human beings to two bodies charged with electricity of different potentials. Isolated from each other the electric forces within them are invisible, but if they come into the right juxtaposition the force is transmuted, and a spark, a glow of burning light arises between them. Such is love.

From the body of the loved one's simple, sweetly coloured flesh, which our immemorial creature instincts urge us to desire, there springs not only the wonder of a new bodily life, but also the enlargement of the horizon of human sympathy and the glow of spiritual understanding which a solitary soul could never have attained alone.

Many reading this may feel conscious that they have had physical union without such spiritual results, perhaps even without an accession of ordinary happiness. If that is so, it can only be because, consciously or unconsciously, they have broken some of the profound laws which govern the love of man and woman. Only by learning to hold a bow correctly can one draw music from a violin: only by obedience to the laws of the lower plane can one step up to the plane above.

CHAPTER II

The Broken Joy

What shall be done to quiet the heart-cry of the world?
How answer the dumb appeal for help we so often divine
below eyes that laugh?—AE in 'The Hero in Man.'

DREAMING of happiness, feeling that at last they have each found the one who will give eternal understanding and tenderness, the young man and maiden marry.[1]

At first, in the time generally called the honeymoon, the unaccustomed freedom and the sweetness of the relation often does bring real happiness. How long does it last? Too often a far shorter time than is generally acknowledged.

---

[1]   In this, and in most of the generalisations found in this book, I am speaking of things as they are in Great Britain. While, to a considerable extent, the same is true of America and the Scandinavian countries, it must be remembered all through that I am speaking of the British and primarily of our educated classes.

In the first joy of their union it is hidden from the two young people that they know little or nothing about the fundamental laws of each other's being. Much of the sex-attraction (not only among human beings, but even throughout the whole world of living creatures) depends upon the differences between the two that pair; and probably taking them all unawares, those very differences which drew them together now begin to work their undoing.

But so long as the first illusion that each understands the other is supported by the thrilling delight of ever-fresh discoveries, the sensations lived through are so rapid and so joyous that the lovers do not realise that there is no firm foundation of real mutual knowledge beneath their feet. While even the happiest pair may know of divergencies about religion, politics, social custom, and opinions on things in general, these, with goodwill, patience, and intelligence on either side, can be ultimately adjusted, because in all such things there is a common meeting ground for the two. Human beings, while differing widely about every conceivable subject in such human relations, have at least *thought* about them, threshed them out, and discussed them openly for generations.

But about the much more fundamental and vital problems of sex, there is a lack of knowledge so abysmal and so universal that its mists and shadowy darkness have affected even the few who lead us, and who are prosecuting research in these subjects. And the two young people begin to suffer from fundamental divergencies, before perhaps they realise that such exist, and with little prospect of ever gaining a rational explanation of them.

Nearly all those whose own happiness seems to be dimmed or broken count themselves exceptions, and comfort themselves with the thought of some of their friends, who, they feel sure, have attained the happiness which they themselves have missed.

It is generally supposed that happy people, like happy nations, have no history—they are silent about their own affairs. Those who talk about their marriage are generally those who have missed the happiness they expected.

True as this may be in general, it is not permanently and profoundly true, and there are people who are reckoned, and still reckon themselves, happy, but who yet unawares reveal the secret disappointment which clouds their inward peace.

Leaving out of account *'femmes incomprises'* and all the innumerable neurotic, super-sensitive, and slightly abnormal people, it still remains an astonishing and tragic fact that *so* large a proportion of marriages lose their early bloom and are to some extent unhappy.

For years many men and women have confided to me the secrets of their lives; and of all the innumerable marriages of which the inner circumstances are known to me, there are tragically few which approach even humanly attainable joy.

Many of those considered by the world, by the relatives, *even by the loved and loving partner,* to be perfectly happy marriages, are secretly shadowed to the more sensitive of the pair.

Where the bride is, as are so many of our educated girls, composed of virgin sweetness shut in ignorance, the man is often the first to create 'the rift within the lute'; but his suffering begins almost simultaneously with hers. The surface freedom of our women has not materially altered, cannot materially alter, the pristine purity of a girl of our northern race. She generally has not even the capacity to imagine the basic facts of physical marriage, and her bridegroom may shock her without knowing that he was doing so. Then, unconscious of the nature, and even perhaps of the existence of his fault, he is bewildered and pained by her inarticulate pain.

Yet I think, nevertheless, it is true that in the early days of marriage the young man is often even more sensitive, more romantic, more easily pained about all ordinary things, and he enters marriage hoping for an even higher degree of spiritual and bodily unity than does the girl or the woman. But the man is more quickly blunted, more swiftly rendered cynical, and is readier to look upon happiness as a Utopian dream than is his mate.

On the other hand, the woman is slower to realise disappointment, and more often by the sex-life of marriage is of the two the more *profoundly* wounded, with a slow corrosive wound that eats into her very being.

Perfect happiness is a unity composed of a myriad essences; and this one supreme thing is exposed to the attacks of countless destructive factors.

Were I to touch upon all the possible sources of marital disappointment and unhappiness, this book would expand into a dozen bulky volumes. As I am addressing those who I assume have read, or can read, other books written upon various ramifications of the subject, I will not discuss the themes which have been handled by many writers, nor deal with abnormalities, which fill so large a part of most books on sex.

In the last few years there has been such an awakening to the realisation of the corrosive horror of all aspects of prostitution that there is no need to labour the point that no marriage can be happy where the husband has, in buying another body, sold his own health with his honour, and is tainted with disease.

Nor is it necessary, in speaking to well-meaning, optimistic young couples, to enlarge upon the obvious dangers of drunkenness, self-indulgence, and the cruder forms of selfishness. It is with the subtler infringements of the fundamental laws we have to deal. And the prime tragedy is that, as a rule, the two young people are both unaware of the existence of such decrees. Yet here, as elsewhere in Nature, the law breaker is punished whether he is aware of the existence of the law he breaks or not.

In the state of ignorance which so largely predominates to-day, the first sign that things are amiss between the two who thought they were entering paradise together, is generally a sense of loneliness, a feeling that the one who was expected to have all in common is outside some experience, some subtle delight, and fails to understand the needs of the loved one. Trivialities are often the first indicators of something which takes its roots unseen in the profoundest depths. The girl may sob for hours over something so trifling that she cannot even put into words its nature, while the young man, thinking that he had set out with his soul's beloved upon an adventure into celestial distances, may find himself apparently up against a barrier in her which appears as incomprehensible as it is frivolous.

Then, so strange is the mystical inter-relation between our bodies, our minds, and our souls, that for crimes committed in ignorance of the dual functions of the married pair, and the laws which harmonise them, the punishments are reaped on planes quite diverse, till new and ever new misunderstandings appear to spring spontaneously from the soil of their mutual contact. Gradually or swiftly each heart begins to hide a sense of boundless isolation. It may be urged that this statement is too sweeping. It is, however, based on innumerable actual lives. I have heard from women whose marriages are looked upon by all as the happiest possible expressions of human felicity, the details of secret pain of which they have allowed their husbands no inkling. Many men will know how they have hidden from their beloved wives a sense of dull disappointment, perhaps at her coldness in the marital embrace, or from the sense that there is in her something elusive which always evades their grasp!

This profound sense of misunderstanding finds readier expression in the cruder and more ordinary natures. The disappointment of the married is expressed not only in innumerable books and plays, but even in comic papers and all our daily gossip.

Now that so many 'movements' are abroad, folk on all sides are emboldened to express the opinion that it is marriage itself which is at fault. Many think that merely by loosening the bonds, and making it possible to start afresh with someone else, their lives would be made harmonious and happy. But often such reformers forget that he or she who knows nothing of the way to make marriage great and beautiful with one partner, is not likely to succeed with another. Only by a reverent study of the Art of Love can the beauty of its expression be realised in linked lives.

And even when once learnt the Art of Love takes *time* to practise. As Ellen Key says, 'Love requires peace, love will dream; it cannot live upon the remnants of our time and our personality.'

There is no doubt that Love loses, in the haste and bustle of the modern turmoil, not only its charm and graces, but some of its vital essence. The evil results of the haste which so infests and poisons us are often felt much more by the woman than by the man. The over-stimulation of city life tends to 'speed up' the man's reactions, but to retard hers. To make matters worse, even for those who have leisure to spend on love-making, the opportunities for peaceful, romantic dalliance are less to-day in a city with its tubes and cinema shows than in woods and gardens where the pulling of rosemary or lavender may be the sweet excuse for the slow and profound mutual rousing of passion. Now physical passion, so swiftly stimulated in man, tends to override all else, and the untutored man seeks but one thing—the accomplishment of desire. The woman, for it is in her nature so to do, forgives the crudeness, but sooner or later her love revolts, probably in secret, and then for ever after, though she may command an outward tenderness, she has nothing within but scorn and loathing for the act which should have been a perpetually recurring entrancement.

CHAPTER V

Mutual Adjustment

'Love worketh no ill to his neighbour.'—ST PAUL.

IN the average man of our race desire knows no season beyond the slight slackening of the winter months and the heightening of spring. Some men have observed in themselves a faintly-marked monthly rhythm; but in the majority of men desire, even if held in stern check, is merely slumbering. It is always present, ever ready to wake at the lightest call, and often so spontaneously insistent as to require perpetual conscious repression.

It would go ill with the men of our race had women retained the wild animals' infrequent seasonal rhythm, and with it her inviolable rights in her own body save at the mating season. Woman, too, has acquired a much more frequent rhythm; but, as it does not equal man's, he has tended to ignore and over-ride it, coercing her at all times and seasons, either by force, or by the even more compelling power of 'divine' authority and social tradition.

If man's desire is perpetual and woman's intermittent; if man's desire naturally wells up every day or every few days, and woman's only every fortnight or every month, it may appear at first sight impossible for the unwarped needs of both natures simultaneously to be satisfied.

The sense that a satisfactory mutual adjustment is not within the realms of possibility has, indeed, obsessed our race for centuries. The result has been that the supposed need of one of the partners has tended to become paramount, and we have established the social traditions of a husband's 'rights' and wifely 'duty'. As one man quite frankly said to me: 'As things are it is impossible for both sexes to get what they want. One *must* be sacrificed. And it is better for society that it should be the woman.'

Nevertheless, the men who consciously sacrifice the women are in a minority. Most men act in ignorance. Our code, however, has blindly sacrificed not only the woman, but with her the happiness of the majority of men, who, in total ignorance of its meaning and results, have grown up thinking that women should submit to regularly frequent, or even nightly, intercourse. For the sake of a few moments of physical pleasure they lose realms of ever-expanding joy and tenderness; and while men and women may not realise the existence of an untrodden paradise, they both suffer, if only half consciously, from being shut out from it.

Before making some suggestions which may help married people to find not only a *via media* of mutual endurance, but a *via perfecta* of mutual joy, it is necessary to consider a few points about the actual nature of man's 'desire.' In the innumerable books addressed to the young which I have read, I have not found one which gives certain points regarding the meaning of the male sex-phenomena which must be grasped before it is possible to give rational guidance to intelligent young men. The general ground plan of our physiology is told to us in youth because it so obviously is right for us to know it accurately and in a clean scientific way, rather than to be perpetually perplexed by fantastic imaginings. But the physiology of our most profoundly disturbing functions is ignored—in my opinion, criminally ignored. To describe the essentials, simple, direct and scientific language is necessary, though it may surprise those who are accustomed only to the hazy vagueness which has led to so much misapprehension of the truth. Every mating man and woman should know the following: The sex organs of a man consist not only of the tissues which give rise to the living, moving, ciliated cells, the *sperms,* and of the penis through which they pass and by means of which they are directed into the proper place for their deposition, the woman's vagina. Associated with these primary and essential structures there are other tissues and glands which have numerous subsidiary but yet very important parts to play; some of which influence almost every organ in the body. Man's penis, when unstimulated, is soft, small and drooping. But when stimulated, either by physical touch which acts through the nerves and muscles directly, or indirectly through messages from the brain, it increases greatly in size, and becomes stiff, turgid and erect. Many men imagine that the turgid condition of an erection is due to the local accumulation of sperms, and that these can only be naturally got rid of by an ejaculation. This is entirely wrong. The enlargement of the penis is not at all due to the presence of actual sperm, but is due to the effects of the nervous reaction on the blood-vessels, leading to the filling, principally of the *veins,* and much less of the arteries. As the blood enters but does not leave the penis, the venous cavities in it fill up with venous blood until the whole is rigid. When rigid this organ is able to penetrate the female entrance, and there the further stimulation calls out the sperms from their storehouses, the seminal vesicles in the testes, and they pass down the channel (the urethra) and are expelled. If this is clear, it will be realised that the stiffening and erection does not *necessarily* call for relief in the ejaculation of sperm. If the veins can empty themselves, as they naturally do when the nervous excitement which restricted them locally passes, the erection will subside without any loss of sperms, by the mere passing back of the locally excessive blood into the ordinary circulatory system. This can happen quite naturally and healthily when the nerves are soothed, either physically or as a result of a sense of mental peace and exaltation. When, on the other hand, the local excitement culminates in the calling up and expulsion of the sperms, after it has once started the ejaculation becomes quite involuntary and the sperms and the secretions associated with them pass out of the system and are entirely lost.

Of what does this loss consist? It is estimated that there are somewhere between two and five hundred million sperms in a single average ejaculation. Each single one of these (in healthy men) is capable of fertilising a woman's egg-cell and giving rise to a new human being. (Thus by a single ejaculation one man might fertilise nearly all the marriageable women in the world!) Each single one of those minute sperms carries countless hereditary traits, and each consists very largely of nuclear plasm—the most highly-specialised and richest substance in our bodies. It is not surprising, therefore, to find that the analysis of the chemical nature of the ejaculated fluid reveals among other things a remarkably high percentage of calcium and phosphoric acid—both precious substances in our organisation.

It is therefore the greatest mistake to imagine that the semen is something to be got rid of *frequently*—all the vital energy and the precious chemical substances which go to its composition can be better utilised by being transformed into other creative work on most days of the month. And so mystic and wonderful are the chemical transformations going on in our bodies that the brain can often set this alchemy in motion, particularly if the brain is helped by *knowledge.* A strong will can often calm the nerves which regulate the blood supply, and order the distended veins of the penis to retract and subside without wasting the semen in an ejaculation.

But while it is good that a man should be able to do this often, it is not good to try to do it always. The very restraint which adds to a man's strength up to a point, taxes his strength when carried beyond it. It is my belief that just sufficient restraint to carry him through the ebb-tides of his wife's sex-rhythm is usually the right amount to give the best strength, vigour, and joy to a man if both are normal people. If the wife has, as I think the majority of healthy, well-fed young women will be found to have, a fortnightly consciousness or unconscious *potentiality* of desire, then the two should find a perfect mutual adjustment in having fort-nightly unions; for this need not be confined to only a single union on such occasion. Many men, who can well practise restraint for twelve or fourteen days, will find that one union only will not then thoroughly satisfy them; and if they have the good fortune to have healthy wives, they will find that the latter, too, have the desire for several unions in the course of a day or two . . . This is what happens when a woman is thoroughly well and vital; her desire recurs during a day or two, sometimes even every few hours if it does not, and sometimes even when it does, receive satisfaction.

Expressed in general terms (which, of course, will not fit everybody) my view may be formulated thus: The mutually best regulation of intercourse in marriage is to have three or four days of repeated unions, followed by about ten days without any unions at all, unless some strong external stimulus has stirred a mutual desire.

I have been interested to discover that the people known to me who have accidentally fixed upon this arrangement of their lives are *happy:* and it should be noted that it fits in with the charts I give which represent the normal, spontaneous feeling of so many women.

There are many women, however, who do not feel, or who may not at first recognise, a second, but have only one time of natural pleasure in sex in each moon-month. Many men of strong will and temperate lives will be able so to control themselves that they can adjust themselves to this more retrained sex-life, as do some with whom I am acquainted. On the other hand, there will be many who find this period too long to live through without using a larger amount of energy in restraining their impulse than is justifiable. It seems to me never justifiable to spend so much energy and will power on restraining natural impulses, that valuable work and intellectual power and poise are made to suffer. If, then, a strongly-sexed husband, who finds it a real loss to his powers of work to endure through twenty-six days of abstinence, should find himself married to a wife whose vitality is so low that she can only take pleasure in physical union once in her moon-month (in some it will be before, in some a little time after, her menstrual flow), he should note carefully the time she is spontaneously happy in their union, and then at any cost restrain himself through the days immediately following, and about a fortnight after her time of desire he should set himself ardently to woo her. Unless she is actually out of health he is more likely then than at any other time to succeed not only in winning her compliance, but also in giving her the proper feeling and attaining mutual ecstasy.

The husband who so restrains himself, even if it is hard to do it, will generally find that he is a thousand-fold repaid not only by the increasing health and happiness of his wife, and the much intenser pleasure he gains from their mutual intercourse, but also by his own added vitality and sense of self-command. A fortnight is not too long for a healthy man to restrain himself with advantage.

Sir Thomas Clouston says ('Before I Wed,' 1913, page 84): 'Nature has also so arranged matters that the more constantly control is exercised the more easy and effective it becomes. It becomes a *habit*. The less control is exercised the greater tendency there is for a desire to become a *craving* of an uncontrollable kind, which is itself of the nature of disease, and means death sooner or later.' This conclusion is not only the result of the intellectual and moral experience of our race, but is supported by physiological experiments.

While a knowledge of the fundamental laws of our being should in the main regulate our lives, so complex are we, so sensitive to a myriad impressions, that clock-work regularity can never rule us.

Even where the woman is strongly sexed, with a well-marked recurrence of desire, which is generally satisfied by fortnightly unions, it may not infrequently happen that, in between these periods, there may be additional special occasions when there springs up a mutual longing to unite. These will generally depend on some event in the lovers' lives which stirs their emotions; some memory of past passion, such as an anniversary of their wedding, or perhaps will be due to a novel, poem, or picture which moves them deeply. If the man she loves plays the part of tender wooer, even at times when her passion would not *spontaneously* arise, a woman can generally be stirred so fundamentally as to give a passionate return. But at the times of her ebb-tides the stimulus will have to be stronger than at the high tides, and it will then generally be found that the appeal must be made even more through her emotional and spiritual nature and less through the physical than usual.

The supreme law for husbands is: Remember that each act of union must be tenderly wooed for and won, and that no union should ever take place unless the woman also desires it and is made physically ready for it. . .

Ellis states that the Queen of Aragon ordained that six times a day was the proper rule in legitimate marriage! So abnormally sexed a woman would to-day probably succeed in killing by exhaustion a succession of husbands, for the man who could match such a desire is rare, though perhaps less exceptional than such a woman.

Though the timing and the frequency of union are the points about which questions are oftenest asked by the ignorant and well-meaning, and are most misunderstood, yet there are other fundamental facts concerning coitus about which even medical men seem surprisingly ignorant. Regarding these, a simple statement of the physiological facts is essential.

An impersonal and scientific knowledge of the structure of our bodies is the surest safeguard against prurient curiosity and lascivious gloating. This knowledge at the back of the minds of the lovers, though not perhaps remembered as such, may also spare the unintentioned cruelty of handling which so readily injures one whose lover is ignorant.

What actually happens in an act of union should be known. After the preliminaries have mutually roused the pair, the stimulated penis, enlarged and stiffened, is pressed into the woman's vagina. Ordinarily when a woman is not stimulated, the walls of this canal, as well as the exterior lips of soft tissue surrounding it, are dry and rather crinkled, and the vaginal opening is smaller than the man's extended penis. But when the woman is what is physiologically called tumescent (that is, when she is ready for union and has been profoundly stirred) these parts are flushed by the internal blood supply and to some extent are turgid like those of the man, while a secretion of mucous lubricates the channel of the vagina. In an ardent woman the vagina may even spontaneously open and close. (So powerful is the influence of thought on our bodily structure, that in some people all these physical results may be brought about by the thought of the loved one, by the enjoyment of tender words and kisses, and the beautiful subtleties of wooing.) It can therefore be readily imagined that when the man tries to enter a woman whom he has *not* wooed to the point of stimulating her natural physical reactions of preparation, he is endeavouring to force his entry through a dry-walled opening too small for it. He may thus cause the woman actual pain, apart from the mental revolt and loathing she is likely to feel for a man who so regardlessly uses her. On the other hand, in the tumescent woman the opening, already naturally expanded, is lubricated by mucous, and all the nerves and muscles are ready to react and easily accept the man's entering organ. This account is of the meeting of two who have been already married. The first union of a virgin girl differs, of course, from all others, for on that occasion the hymen is broken. One would think that every girl who was about to be married would be told of this necessary rupturing of the membrane and the temporary pain it will cause her; but even still large numbers of girls are allowed to marry in complete and cruel ignorance.

It should be realised that a man does not woo and win a woman once for all when he marries her: *he must woo her before every separate act of coitus,* for each act corresponds to a marriage as other creatures know it. Wild animals are not so foolish as man; a wild animal does not unite with his female without the wooing characteristic of his race, whether by stirring her by a display of his strength in fighting another male, or by exhibiting his beautiful feathers or song. And we must not forget that the wild animals are assisted by nature;

they generally only woo just at the season when the female is beginning to feel natural desire. But man, who wants his mate all out of season as well as in it, has a double duty to perform, and must himself rouse, charm, and stimulate her to the local readiness which would have been to some extent naturally prepared for him had he waited till her own desire welled up.

To render a woman ready before uniting with her is not only the merest act of humanity to save her pain, but is of value from the man's point of view, for (unless he is one of those relatively few abnormal and diseased variants who delight only in rape) the man gains an immense increase of sensation from the mutuality thus attained, and the health of both the man and the woman is most beneficially affected.

Assuming now that the two are in the closest mental and spiritual, as well as sensory harmony: in what position should the act be consummated? Men and women, looking into each other's eyes, kissing tenderly on the mouth, with their arms round each other, meet face to face. And that position is symbolic of the coming together of the two who meet together gladly.

It seems incredible that to-day educated men should be found who—apparently on theological grounds—refuse to countenance any other position. Yet one wife told me that she was crushed and nearly suffocated by her husband, so that it took her hours to recover after each union, but that 'on principle' he refused to attempt any other position than the one he chose to consider normal. Mutual well-being should be the guide for each pair.

It is perhaps not generally realised how great are the variations of size, shape, and position of all the sex parts of the body in different individuals, yet they differ more even than the size and characters of all the features of the face and hands. It happens, therefore, that the position which suits most people is unsatisfactory for others. Some, for instance, can only benefit by union when both are lying on their sides.

Though medically this is generally considered unfavourable or prohibitive for conception, yet I know women who have had several children and whose husbands always used this position. In this matter every couple should find out for themselves which of the many possible positions best suits them *both*.

When the two have met and united, the usual result is that, after a longer or shorter interval, the man's mental and physical stimulation reaches a climax in sensory intoxication and in the ejaculation of semen. Where the two are perfectly adjusted, the woman simultaneously reaches the crisis of nervous and muscular reactions very similar to his. This mutual orgasm is extremely important, but in many cases the man's climax comes so swiftly that the woman's reactions are not nearly ready, and she is left without it. Though in some instances the woman may have one or more crises before the man achieves his, it is, perhaps, hardly an exaggeration to say that 70 or 80 per cent of our married women (in the middle classes) are deprived of the full orgasm through the excessive speed of the husband's reactions, or through some mal-adjustment of the relative shapes and positions of the organs. So deep-seated, so profound, are woman's complex sex-instincts as well as her organs, that in rousing them the man is rousing her whole body and soul. And this takes time. More time, indeed, than the average, uninstructed husband gives to it. Yet woman has at the surface a small vestigeal organ called the clitoris, which corresponds morphologically to the man's penis, and which, like it, is extremely sensitive to touch-sensations. This little crest, which lies anteriorly between the inner lips round the vagina, enlarges when the woman is really tumescent, and by the stimulation of movement it is intensely roused and transmits this stimulus to every nerve in her body. But even after a woman's dormant sex-feeling is aroused and all the complex reactions of her being have been set in motion, it may even take as much as from ten to twenty minutes of actual physical union to consummate her feeling, while two or three minutes often completes the union for a man who is ignorant of the need to control his reactions so that both may experience the added benefit of a mutual crisis to love.

A number of well-meaning people demand from men absolute 'continence' save for procreation only. They overlook the innumerable physiological reactions concerned in the act, as well as the subtle spiritual alchemy of it, and propound the view that 'the opposition to continence, save for procreation only, has but one argument to put forward, and that is appetite, selfishness.' *(The Way of God in Marriage.)*

I maintain, however, that it should be realised that the complete act of union is a triple consummation. It symbolises, and at the same time actually enhances, the spiritual union; there are a myriad subtleties of soul-structures which are compounded in this alchemy. At the same time the act gives the most intense physical pleasure and benefit which the body can experience, and it is a *mutual,* not a selfish, pleasure and profit, more calculated than anything else to draw out an unspeakable tenderness and understanding in both partakers of this sacrament; while, thirdly, it is the act which gives rise to a new life by rendering possible the fusion of one of the innumerable male sperms with the female egg-cell.

It often happens nowadays that, dreading the expense and the physical strain of child-bearing for his wife, the husband practises what is called *coitus interruptus*—that is, he withdraws just before the ejaculation, but when he is already so stimulated that the ejaculation has become involuntary. In this way the semen is spent, but, as it does not enter the wife's body, fertilisation and, consequently, procreation cannot take place. This practice, while it may have saved the woman the anguish of bearing unwanted children, is yet very harmful to her, and is to be deprecated. It tends to leave the woman in 'mid-air' as it were; to leave her stimulated and unsatisfied, and therefore it has a very bad effect on her nerves and general health, particularly if it is done frequently. The woman, too, loses the advantage (and I am convinced that it is difficult to overstate the physiological advantage) of the partial absorption of the man's secretions, which must take place through the large tract of internal epithelium with which they come in contact. If, as physiology has already proved is the case, the internal absorption of secretions from the sex organs plays so large a part in determining the health and character of remote parts of the body, it is extremely likely that the highly stimulating secretion of man's semen can and does penetrate and affect the woman's whole organism. Actual experiment has shown that iodine placed in the vagina in solution is so quickly absorbed by the epithelial walls that in an hour it has penetrated the system and is even being excreted. It still remains, however, for scientific experiments to be devised which will enable us to study the effects of the absorption of substances from the semen. On the other hand, *coitus interruptus* is not always harmful for the man, for he has the complete sex-act, though a good many men think its effects on them are undesirable, and it may lead to lack of desire or even impotence toward his wife in a man who practises it with her, or, on the other hand, to a too swift fresh desire from the lack of complete resolution of nervous tension. It is certainly bad when its safety from consequences induces him to frequent indulgence, for thus wastefully to scatter what should be *creative power* is to reduce his own vitality and power of work. By those who have a high appreciation of the value of their creative impulse, and who wish to know the mutual pleasure and enhancement of sex-union without wasting it, this method should not be practised.

It should never be forgotten that without the discipline of control there is no lasting delight in erotic feeling. The fullest delight, even in a purely physical sense, can *only* be attained by those who curb and direct their natural impulses.

Dr Saleeby's words are appropriate in this connection (Introduction to Forel's 'Sexual Ethics,' 1908): 'Professor Forel speaks of subduing the sexual instinct. I would rather speak of transmuting it. The direct method of attack is often futile, always necessitous of effect, but it is possible for us to transmute our sex-energy into higher forms in our individual lives, thus justifying the evolutionary and physiological contention that it is the source of the higher activities of man, of moral indignation, and of the "restless energy" which has changed the surface of the earth.'

Forel says ('The Sexual Question,' 1908): 'Before engaging in a lifelong union, a man and woman ought to explain to each other their sexual feelings so as to avoid deception and incompatibility later on.' This would be admirable advice were it possible for a virgin girl to know much about the reactions and effects upon her mind and body of the act of coitus, but she does not. Actually it often takes several years for eager and intelligent couples fully to probe themselves and to discover the extent and meaning of the immensely profound physiological and spiritual results of marriage. Yet it is true that a noble frankness would save much misery when, as happens not infrequently, one or other of the pair marry with the secret determination to have no children.

So various are we all as individuals, so complex all the reactions and inter-actions of sex relations, that no hard-and-fast rule can be laid down. Each couple, after marriage, must study themselves, and the lover and the beloved must do what best serves them both and gives them the highest degree of mutual joy and power. There are, however, some laws which should be inviolable. Their details can be gathered from the preceding pages, and they are summed up in the words: 'Love worketh no ill to the beloved.'

CHAPTER XI

The Glorious Unfolding

Let knowledge grow from more to more, but more of
reverence in us dwell.

TENNYSON.

WE are surrounded in this world by processes and
transmutations so amazing that were they not taking place
around us hourly they would be scouted as impossible
imaginings.

A mind must be dull and essentially lacking in
wonderment which, without amazement, can learn for the
first time that the air we breathe, apparently so uniform in its
invisible unity, is in reality composed of two principal, and
several other, gases. The two gases, however, are but mixed
as wine may be with water, and each gas by itself is a
colourless air, visually like that mixture of the two which we
call the atmosphere.

Much greater is the miracle of the composition of water.
It is made of only two gases, one of them a component of the
air we breathe, and the other similarly invisible and
odourless, but far lighter. These two invisible gases, when
linked in a proportion proper to their natures, fuse and are no
longer ethereal and invisible, but precipitate in a new
substance—water.

The waves of the sea with their thundering power, the
sparkling tides of the river buoying the ships, are but the
transmuted resultants of the union of two invisible gases.
And this, in its simplest terms, is a parable of the infinitely
complex and amazing transmutations of married love.

Ellis expresses the strange mystery of one of the
physical sides of love when he says:

What has always baffled men in the contemplation of sexual love is the seeming inadequacy of its cause, the immense discrepancy between the necessarily circumscribed regions of mucous membrane which is the final goal of such love and the sea of world-embracing emotions to which it seems the door, so that, as Remy de Gourmont has said, 'the mucous membranes, by an ineffable mystery, enclose in their obscure folds all the riches of the infinite.' It is a mystery before which the thinker and the artist are alike overcome.

To me, however, the recent discoveries of physiology seem to afford a key which may unlock a chamber of the mystery and admit us to one of the halls of the palace of truth. The hormones in each individual body pour from one organ and affect another, and thus influence the whole character of the individual's life processes. The visible secretions and the most subtle essences which pass during union between man and woman, affect the lives of each and are essentially vital to each other. As I see them, the man and the woman are each organs, parts, of the other. And in the strictest scientific, as well as in a mystical, sense they *together* are a single unit, an individual entity. There is a *physiological* as well as a spiritual truth in the words 'they twain shall be one flesh.'

In love it is not only that the yearning of the bonds of affinity to be satisfied is met by the linking with another, but that out of this union there grows a new and unprecedented creation.

In this I am not speaking of the bodily child which springs from the love of its parents, but of the super-physical entity created by the perfect union in love of man and woman. Together, united by the love bonds which hold them, they are a new and wondrous thing surpassing, and different from, the arithmetical sum of them both when separate.

So seldom has the perfection of this new creation been experienced, that we are still far short even of imagining its full potentialities, but that it must have mighty powers we dimly realise.

Youths and maidens stirred by the attraction of love, feel hauntingly and inarticulately that there is before them an immense and beautiful experience: feel as though in union with the beloved there will be added powers of every sort which have no measure in terms of the ordinary unmated life.

These prophetic dreams, if they are not true of each individual life, are yet true of the race as a whole. For in the dreams of youth to-day is a foreshadowing of the reality of the future.

So accustomed have we recently become to accept one aspect of organic evolution, that we tend to see in youth only a recapitulation of our race's history. The well-worn phrase 'Ontogeny repeats Phylogeny' has helped to concentrate our attention on the fact that the young in their development, in ourselves as in the animals, go through many phases which resemble the stages through which the whole race must have passed in the course of its evolution.

While this is true, there is another characteristic of youth: It is prophetic!

The dreams of youth, which each young heart expects to see fulfilled in its own life, seem so often to fade unfulfilled. But that is because the wonderful powers of youth are not supplied with the necessary tool—knowledge. And so potentialities, which could have worked miracles, are allowed to atrophy and die.

But as humanity orients itself more truly, more and more will the knowledge and experience of the whole race be placed at the disposal of all youth on its entry into life.

Then that glorious upspringing of the racial ideal, which finds its expression in each unspoiled generation of youth, will at last meet with a store of knowledge sufficient for its needs, and will find ready as a tool to its hand the accumulated and sifted wisdom of the race.

Then youth will be spared the blunders and the pain and the unconscious self-destruction that to-day leaves scarcely anyone untouched.

In my own life, comparatively short and therefore lacking in experience though it be, I have known both personally and vicariously so much anguish that might have been prevented by knowledge. This impels me not to wait till my experience and researches are complete, and my life and vital interest are fading, but to hand on at once those gleanings of wisdom I have already accumulated which may help the race to understand itself. Hence I conclude this little book, for, though incomplete, it contains some of the vital things youth should be told.

In all life activities, house-building, hunting or any other, where intellectual and oral tradition comes in, as it does with the human race, 'instinct' tends to die out. Thus the human mother is far less able to manage her baby without instruction than is a cat her kittens; although the human mother at her best has, in comparison with the cat, an infinitude of duties toward, and influences over, her child.

A similar truth holds in relation to marriage. The century-long following of various 'civilised' customs has not only deprived our young people of most of the instinctive knowledge they might have possessed, but has given rise to innumerable false and polluting customs.

Though many write on the art of managing children, few have anything to say about the art of marriage, save those who have some dogma, often theological or subversive of natural law, to proclaim.

Any fundamental truth regarding marriage is rendered immeasurably difficult to ascertain because of the immense ranges of variety in human beings, even of the same race, many of which result from the artificial conditions and the unnatural stimuli so prevalent in what we call civilisation.

To attempt anything like a serious study of marriage in all its varieties would be a monumental work. Those who have even partially undertaken it have tended to become entangled in a maze of abnormalities, so that the needs of the normal, healthy, romantic person have been overlooked.

Each pair, therefore, has tended to repeat the blunders from which it might have been saved, and to stumble blindly in a maze of difficulties which are not the essential heritage of humanity, but are due to the unreasoning folly of our present customs.

I have written this book for those who enter marriage normally and healthily, and with optimism and hope.

If they learn its lessons they may be saved from some of the pitfalls in which thousands have wrecked their happiness, but they must not think that they will thereby easily attain the perfection of marriage. There are myriad subtleties in the adjustment of any two individuals.

Each pair must, using the tenderest and most delicate touches, sound and test each other, learning their way about the intricacies of each other's hearts.

Sometimes, with all the knowledge and the best will in the world, two who have married find that they cannot fuse their lives; of this tragedy I have not here anything to say; but ordinary unhappiness would be less frequent than it is were the tenderness of *knowledge* applied to the problem of mutual adjustment from the first day of marriage.

All the deepest and highest forces within us impel us to evolve an ever nobler and tenderer form of life-long monogamy as our social ideal. While the thoughtful and tenderhearted must seek, with ever greater understanding, to ease and comfort those who miss this joyful natural development, reformers in their zeal for side-issues must not forget the main growth of the stock. The beautiful sense for love in the hearts of the young should be encouraged, and they should have access to the knowledge of how to cultivate it, instead of being diverted by the clamour for 'freedom' to destroy it.

Disillusioned middle age is apt to look upon the material side of the marriage relation, to see its solid surface in the cold, dull light of everyday experience; while youth, irradiated by the glow of its dreams, is unaware how its aerial and celestial phantasies are broken and shattered when unsuspectingly brought up against the hard facts of physical reality.

The transmutation of material facts by celestial phantasies is to some extent within the power of humanity, even the imperfect humanity of to-day.

When knowledge and love together go to the making of each marriage, the joy of *that new unit, the pair* will reach from the physical foundations of its bodies to the heavens where its head is crowned with stars.

Wise Parenthood

(1918)

Dedicated to all who wish to see our race grow in strength and beauty.

CHAPTER I

> "I think, dearest Uncle, you cannot *really* wish me to be the *'Mamma d'une nombreuse famille,'* for I think you will see the great inconvenience a *large* family would be to us all, and particularly to the country, independent of the hardship and inconvenience to myself. Men never think, at least seldom think, what a hard task it is for us women to go through this *very often."* — QUEEN VICTORIA in a letter to the King of the Belgians, January 15, 1841.

A FAMILY of healthy happy children should be the joy of every pair of married lovers. To-day more than ever the course of duty and delight coincide for those who have health and love in their homes. For to-day as never before the world needs the products of sound and beautiful love, and though these range from the intangible aroma of peace and happiness which a rightly wedded pair radiate, through an infinite variety of spiritual and physical results, the most vital and the most potentially valuable to the community are the children.

Whatever theory of the transmission of characteristics scientists may ultimately adopt, there can be little doubt in the minds of rational people that heredity *does* tell, and that children who descend from a double line of healthy and intelligent parents are better equipped to face whatever difficulties in their environment may later arise than are children from unsound stock. As Sir James Barr said in the *British Medical journal,* 1918: "There is no equality in nature among children nor among adults, and if there is to be a much-needed improvement in the race, we must breed from the physically, morally and intellectually fit."

Nevertheless, the happiness which children should be in a home depends less on a conscious sense of civic virtue (though that may be a factor), than on an acute and warm personal feeling of the parents towards each other. Every man who finds beauty and goodness in his wife must feel a keen desire to repeat that beauty and goodness throughout all time, and every woman who has picked her mate freely, and because she thought him a knight among men, must long to see his characteristics reproduced, so that the world should not lose the imprint of his splendour when the inevitable happens and he has to pass. Indeed, one may almost take it as an axiom when dealing with true love that the pair do feel thus towards each other, and consequently desire children, unless they are aware that either is stricken by some inherent weakness or disease which might reappear in the child. Then they must refrain from parenthood out of a sense of duty and pity towards the unborn.

Nature herself provided that men and women should delight in meeting. Given a loving married pair in normal health, and unsophisticated in any way, there is seldom any lack of children around them after they have been wedded for some years. This is what is still described as the "natural" condition of affairs, and in these days of sophistication in so-called "civilisation," some reformers urge a return to Nature and an unregulated birth-rate.

If, however, the course of "nature" is allowed to run unguided, babies come in general too quickly for the resources of most, and particularly of city-dwelling, families, and the parents as well as the children consequently suffer. Wise parents therefore guide nature, and control the conception of the desired children so as to space them in the way best adjusted to what health, wealth, and happiness they have to give. The object of this book is to tell prospective parents how best to do this, and to hand on to them in a concise form what help science can give on this vital subject.

This is not an attempt to present complete arguments to show the racial and national necessity for the Control of Conception: various aspects of this theme have been presented by others.

Recently valuable expositions of the supreme importance to humanity of a wise use of the control of conception have been made from many different points of view and by various distinguished people. Doubtless much more remains to be said, for there are many who are still ignorant, and consequently prejudiced against the greatest of the steps humanity can take next in its evolution; but this is not the place to deal with the wider aspects of the subject.

That a large proportion of intelligent and thoughtful married couples are practising at the present moment some method or other of the control of conception is beyond dispute. In Lord Dawson of Penn's speech before the Church Congress at Birmingham in 1921 he said: "I will put forward with confidence the view that birth control is here to stay. It is an established fact, and for good or evil has to be accepted. Although the extent of its application can be and is being modified, no denunciations will abolish it." The question before us, therefore, is not whether or no some knowledge of contraceptives should be allowed; it is already established. General dissatisfaction with most of the methods used is however prevalent; and this dissatisfaction is not being alleviated, because there is also a widespread ignorance of satisfactory methods, even on the part of medical practitioners. Numbers of people who are practising and have been practising the control of conception by various means for years, are in urgent need of a better method than any known to them. The following pages are written for them.

. . . What we are here concerned with is the fact that contraceptive methods of all sorts are now so widely used that it is high time serious attention should be devoted to the subject. People should not be employing anything less satisfactory than the best now obtainable; but, unless they are given the best, they will assuredly use some less desirable means.

I will give a quotation from one of our most ardent social reformers. The Rev. Sir J. Marchant, Secretary of the Birth Rate Commission and Director of the National Council of Public Morals, in his book, "Birth Rate and Empire," says as follows (pp. 144-146):

If, then, the volitional control of births within the married state has become a normal proceeding, if it is fast losing its apparent indelicacy, if it is spoken about without raising vicious passions, if it is becoming the "correct thing" to do . . . we must give up the futile attempt to keep young people in the dark and the assumption that they are ignorant of notorious facts. We cannot, if we would, stop the spread of sexual knowledge; and, if we could do so, we should only make matters infinitely worse. This is the second decade of the twentieth century, not the early Victorian period . . . It is, then, no longer a question of knowing or not knowing. We have to disabuse our middle-aged minds of that fond delusion. Our young people know more than we did when we began our married lives, and sometimes as much as we know ourselves, even now. So that we need not continue to shake our few remaining hairs in simulating feelings of surprise and horror. It might have been better for us if we had been more enlightened. And if our discussion of this problem is to be of any real use, we must at the outset reconcile ourselves to the facts that the birth-rate is voluntarily controlled, that brides and bridegrooms know how it is done, and many will certainly do it. Certain persons who instruct us in these matters may hold up their pious hands and whiten their frightened faces as they cry out in the public squares against "this vice," but they only make themselves ridiculous. Their influence in stemming the tide is nearly *nil.*

The Rev. Sir J. Marchant says, "Brides and bridegrooms know how it is done." That is true. They know some, perhaps several, ways of securing voluntary instead of involuntary parenthood, but very few have precise and satisfactory knowledge of, or understand the reasons against, many of the methods which are recommended to them either by medical men or by friends who, as ignorant as they themselves, have been in the habit of using methods described as "harmless," simply because they do no gross and obvious injury.

Many things are reckoned "harmless" which are nevertheless far from satisfactory. Let me take an illustration from another aspect of our lives. Every medical man would consider doses of a half-teaspoonful of ammoniated quinine as not only harmless but beneficial to a patient suffering from influenza. Nevertheless, some even in normal health find that a few such doses upset the digestion for several weeks. It is true that in an influenza epidemic it may be more important to order quinine than to think about people's digestions, and in this sense quinine is not only "harmless" but beneficial. There are many parallels to this in the use of various kinds of preventives which are described as "harmless."

It is amazing that medical and physiological science should have so neglected research on this most vital subject, and that a more perfect procedure should not yet have been devised: it is perhaps more amazing that the reactions and results of the methods now widely used should not have been thoroughly studied and understood. The methods which I have to suggest are not yet the ideal, but they are much simpler, more healthful and less disillusioning than those most in vogue before this book was written. I am glad to think it has materially changed current practice.

After giving the details necessary for the comprehension and employment of the best methods which I can recommend, I shall mention one or two others of those in general use, with reasons why I think them inadvisable save in very special circumstances. The large number of other and still less satisfactory means employed will not be touched upon at all, as this is not a monographic dissertation, but an attempt to be helpful by presenting, if not the ideal, at any rate the good in place of the less good or actually bad.

A few fortunate people who really understand their own physiology, or by happy instinct have chanced upon the right use of their bodies and have been in the habit of practising satisfactory methods, may say or think that such simple and direct instruction as follows is not needed. I have, however, overwhelming evidence and experience that ignorance is rife even in the very places where knowledge might be expected to hold sway. For some time past, scarcely a day has gone by without my receiving letter after letter from people who have long been married, from people who have consulted physicians, from people who have tried many experiments, and who are yet ignorant of any really *satisfactory* means of achieving what they have been perforce achieving in unsatisfactory ways. I once asked a medical woman who had had a practice for fifteen years what method she would advise: she knew of no method whatever. A well-known doctor in London, who for twenty years had had a general and important family practice, asked me if I could tell him of any method other than the sheath, which was the only one he knew, as his patients were inquiring and he did not know what to tell them. Many married couples, who are even told by the doctor that for the wife to have another child would be fatal, are at the same time not told any rational method of prevention. With variations depending on the temperament of the writer, I get appeals one after the other saying: "We have asked our doctor, but he tells us nothing which is of any use. We have therefore to go on using this, that, or the other method, which we feel to be unsatisfactory, because we do not know what else to do." In the pages which follow they will find an account of the physiological reactions of various methods and will thus be able to use the means best suited to their own circumstances.

Some churchmen recommend and some demand "absolute continence," save when a child is desired as a result of union. Where the mated pair are young, normal, and in love, such advice is not only impracticable, it is detrimental. Under such conditions a rigid and enforced abstinence, even where it is not directly injurious to health, may yet have as harmful effects as incontinence. The capacities and requirements of people vary greatly, and no universal rule can apply to all. Other clerics and ascetic-minded laymen sometimes disguise (perhaps even deceiving themselves) "absolute continence" under the more popular term of "self-control," which has a noble sound, and is liable, by credulous audiences, to be applauded . . . But "self-control" will not limit the numbers of the family unless it is so extensive that its correct description is total abstinence extended over years," and this, as most medical men now agree, is not conducive to the physical well-being, or the mental harmony of a home composed of normal, strong and healthy young people, however suitable it may be for those ageing or of weak vitality. On the one side "absolute continence," and on the other an easy self-indulgence, are in married life equally to be condemned. In either of these two quagmires disasters lie in great variety. The narrow and safe path between them is a wise, reasoned and controlled use of the most intimate and sacred functions of the body.

Though for general guidance the suggestion which I have made, particularly in Chapter V of "Married Love," may be of service, yet each pair must find out for themselves the point where self-control becomes an object in itself and detrimental to health and vitality, and where on the other hand the expression of love begins to slide into a too facile indulgence.

My object is not to make sex-experience a danger-free indulgence, but to raise the sense of responsibility, the standard of self-control and knowledge which goes with maturity, and consequently the ultimate health and happiness of those who mate. It should be understood by the man, who is in general the more active partner, that he has to consider not only himself but his mate, and that *the only right rule in marriage is that which gives the greatest sum total of health and happiness to the two concerned, for the benefit of the nation and the race. To achieve this, most men will have to exercise a fine self-control, truly ennobling and strengthening both to mind and body.*

A knowledge of the means of prevention of conception may co-exist with low standards of living and personal hygiene, but even then such knowledge may save the next generation the misery of being hurled into wretched conditions, and may save the community the cost of maintaining anti-social lives.

Some, who would otherwise welcome the spread of knowledge on this important subject, fear an increase of promiscuous relations as a result. It appears, however, that the type of person who desires to lead an irregular life has long had access to sufficient information to satisfy such requirements, while the virtuous mother has been helpless in her ignorance of how to control her motherhood in the interests of her children. Daily experience at the Birth Control Clinic bears this out in a convincing manner.

Hundreds of worn and wretchedly over-burdened mothers have applied for the help given by knowledge, but not a couple of flighty young people. The latter can get crude information from their companions.

Those who would debar the personally selfish from the knowledge of such methods of control, forget that it is just by those who do not trouble to *prevent* evils that the worst and most disastrous attempts are made to overtake the evils they themselves originated. I do not wish in this book to speak of the prevalence and horror of the poor and ignorant woman's attempts at early abortions: the story would be too heartrending, and is out of place in this little book, which is one of help and guidance.

Destructive of the health of both mother and child are the frantic efforts of women "caught," prematurely after a birth, or too frequently in their lives, by undesired motherhood. The desolating effects of abortion and attempted abortion can only be exterminated by a sound knowledge of the control of conception. In this my message coincides with that of all the Churches in condemning utterly the taking of even an embryonic life.

Alas that so many ignorant women do not realise the difference between the control of conception and abortion, and for want of knowledge of the former are ruining their health and pouring money into the pockets of unscrupulous firms which sell "pills."

CHAPTER II

"All turns on what we say is included under divine law. If it is *de jure divino,* then there is no power to modify it; but if any portion is not, then there is power."

DOES divine law condemn scientific methods of controlling conception? It does not. And Christ never condemned parental control and voluntary parenthood.

The Churches, long after His words were spoken, concocted various views of the matter by combining the Pauline attitude toward sex with various Old Testament verses. But no Church, not even the Roman Catholic, has ever yet had a permanent, a logical, or a racially ennobling code of teaching on the subject. The pressure of public opinion is continually forcing the Churches in this, as in other matters, to shift their ground. Alas! While they endeavour to instruct and legislate, they do not lead.

The Memorandum of the Bishops of the Anglican Catholic Church, the doctrine of the Roman Catholic Church, the pronouncement in congress of the main body of Christian Nonconformists, and the Jewish Church, have all very similarly condemned what they call "artificial" methods. The Roman Catholic Church in particular is the most unyielding in its total condemnation of the use of scientific aid in controlling the production of children, although it—like the other Churches—concedes the *principle* of the justifiability of control in some circumstances. To concede the principle, even while condemning the best methods of effecting such control, is to deny the uses of intellectual progress. The stricter members of the Churches obey their edicts; or, with uneasy or unhappy consciences, disobey because they must, or because their training and intelligence teach them that they should make use of what scientific knowledge is available for their help. Hence numbers of Roman Catholics defy the priests or conceal from them the fact that they use methods of control. An interesting example of a particularly self-reliant and brave Roman Catholic who not only privately but openly defied his priest and publicly advocated birth control is reported in his own words in the *Birth Control News* for April, 1927, vol. v, No. 12. Some priests permit methods and themselves deny the authority of the Church, all of which indicates the nation's hunger for intelligent help on lines suited to modern conditions.

The wisdom of the Churches is ancient and pre-scientific: humanity to-day is modern and lives under increasingly "artificial" conditions: only the divinely-given everlasting truths are eternal, and on these the Churches must base their authority. Are any such divine laws given to the Churches about the Control of Conception?

I answer—None.

The Churches, old and wise, gave suitable advice on sex matters in the early days, and now, confusing their own ancient wisdom with the very word of God, they give to-day similar advice, which is no longer wise.

In respect of the control of conception and general guidance concerning sex unions, the so-called Christian ethic (which incidentally goes back to Genesis for its origin, see page 411 of the First Report of the Birth Rate Commission), has for long neglected some of the highest potentialities of marriage. By chaining it to a low individualism, ignorant or forgetful that "they twain shall be one flesh," and that the married pair is not merely a couple of individuals, whose individual souls may achieve perdition or salvation, the greater truth has been hidden. I maintain that a married couple is a welded pair, a higher unit, whose existence and potentialities on this planet depend largely upon the physical condition of the material body of each of the pair, and of its interplay and exchanges, which are jeopardised without the knowledge how best to control the production of children.

The insistence sometimes made in the name of Christian "morality," that the act of physical union should take place only for the procreation of children, ignores profound physical and religious truths.

On physiological, moral, and religious grounds, therefore, I advocate the restrained sacramental and rhythmic performance of the marriage rites of physical union, throughout the whole married life, as an act of supreme value in itself, separate and distinct from its value as a basis for the procreation of children.

That being so, some knowledge of scientific methods of controlling conception becomes not only useful but of the highest—even of religious—significance.

Consider what is entailed in calling forth into existence new souls, each immortal, as all Churches maintain. This is surely one of the profoundest and most essential ways in which the Church can meet and guide humanity. Could any more exalted and more wonderful opportunity be given to the Churches than to see that the souls thus started upon their journeys, endowed with immortal power to serve or disserve God, should be brought forth in love and at such times as will give them every opportunity for complete human equipment?

The Churches, however, offer to serious and inquiring parents who can rear no more children only the alternatives of total and enforced abstinence, and the so-called "natural" method of consciously timing what should be a spontaneous natural impulse of love to those periods supposed to be "safe." Both these methods I condemn for general use, although they may suit some individual needs. Both thwart what is a high and God-given impulse, and in my opinion consequently both these practices are at times essentially immoral, almost as immoral as forcing sickly and unwanted children upon an unwilling mother and an overburdened world.

Marriage is a great and profound thing, and has a deep spiritual and physical significance apart from and in addition to being the basis of parenthood. And both these practices, allowed as the only means of birth control by the Churches, strike at the roots of the perfect marriage. The common folk who disobey and disregard this advice of the Churches, however wrong they are in their *methods,* are right in their deep instinct to obey God's ordinance that the twain shall be one flesh. There is, for this aspect of the subject, "A New Gospel."

The divine law on this great subject has not yet been pronounced finally. The Churches have hitherto based their standard of social morality concerning it on human pronouncements. That being so, religious people should welcome the human understanding of those who to-day most seriously study the question in order to help forward the race in its material journey through space. Science, in reverent hands, may to-day on such a theme more nearly reach divine law than the Churches have yet done.

That this is being felt, even among the leaders of the Church, may be gathered from such writings as those of the Dean of St. Paul's, and the published statement by the Bishop of Birmingham *(The Times,* April 8, 1919) where he said: "Morally, as well as eugenically, it was right for people in certain circumstances to use harmless means to control the birth-rate . . . It was immoral to avoid having children from selfish motives, but it was surely also immoral to have child after child under circumstances which, humanly speaking, were such as to render the proper upbringing of such children impossible."

CHAPTER III

BEFORE entering into the exact structural and medical details of the material methods advisable for those who wish to control the birth of their children, I should like to say a few words on the general subject in its relation to the normal life of the married pair.

I sincerely hope that those who propose to read this little book will *first* read my "Married Love," because the whole complex experience of married life is so interwoven with the sex act, and consequent children, that it is almost impossible to isolate the one thing, namely, the controlling of conception, and discuss that by itself without distorting its relation to the whole of life and appearing to lay stress on the minor details rather than on the greater themes. My object in the following pages is, in the interests both of the pair and of society, to spread what little light science has already thrown upon the subject, so that each pair may not only themselves be healthy and happy, but may bring forth children for the race, who have the best chance which that pair can give them of health and beauty and happiness. From a variety of causes our race is weakened by an appallingly high percentage of unfit weaklings and diseased individuals. It is perhaps only to be expected that the more conscientious, the more thrifty, and the more lovingly desirous to do the best for their children people are, the more do they restrict their families, in the interests both of the children they have and of the community which would otherwise be burdened by their offspring did they not themselves adequately provide for them. Those who are less conscientious, less full of forethought, and less able to provide for the children they bear, and more willing to accept public aid directly and indirectly, are more reckless in the production of large families. Of course there are many individual exceptions, but they do not affect the general tendency. These facts are most significantly borne out by the statistics of the birth-rates of different types of people. For instance, in the Census Report for 1911 (as published and analysed in 1912), we find that the total birth-rate per thousand married men under 55 years old is 162 ; but that the birthrate for the upper and educated classes on this basis is only 119, while that of comparatively unskilled workmen is 213 and over. The detailed analysis of trades and occupations is most interesting, and should be read in conjunction with a memory of the wages and social environment of the various homes. Reckoning per thousand married men below 55 years old, the average number of children is as follows:—

Anglican clergy	101
Other ministers of religion	96
Teachers, professors, etc.	95
Doctors	103
Authors, editors, etc.	104
Policemen	153
Postmen	159
Carmen	207
Dock labourers	231
Barmen	234
Miners	258
"General labourers"	438

The above figures apply only to children born of average married people; when the vicious and feeble-minded people reproduce, they do so more recklessly.

It is found, in short, that the numbers of our population increasingly tend to be made up from the less thrifty and the less conscientious. Were this only a superficial matter, it would concern the race but little, but it is penetratingly profound and far-reaching. The thriftless who breed so rapidly tend by that very fact to bring forth children who are weakened and handicapped by physical as well as mental warping and weakness, and at the same time to demand their support from the sound and thrifty. It is indeed most serious for any race when (as was pointed out in 1918 in *The Times*, of the British then) less than half the population is "physically fit," even when fitness is judged by the comparatively low standard of present-day needs. Moreover we must remember that this half is not free and untrammelled, but is burdened by the partial support and upkeep of the unfit portion of the population, and hence is less able to support children of its own good type than it would be were the incapables nonexistent. Hence only children with the chance of attaining strong, beautiful and intelligent maturity should be conceived. This can only be when the whole relation of each married pair is rightly adjusted, and therefore it is my earnest request that those who have not yet read "Married Love" will lay this book aside until they have done so.

Radiant Motherhood (1920)

CHAPTER I

The Lover's Dream

> So every spirit, as it is most pure,
> And hath in it the more of heauenly
> light,
> So it the fairer bodie doth procure
> To habit in, and it more fairely dight,
> With chearefull grace and
> amiable sight.
> For of the soule the bodie forme
> doth take:
> For soule *is* forme, and doth the
> bodie make.
> SPENCER: *An Hymne in honour of
> Beautie.*

EVERY lover desires a child. Those who imagine the contrary, and maintain that love is purely selfish, know only of the lesser types of love. The supreme love of true mates always carries with it the yearning to perpetuate the exquisite quality of its own being, and to record, through the glory of its mutual creation, other lives yet more beautiful and perfect.

Existence being such a difficult compromise between our dreams and the material facts of the world, this desire may sometimes be thwarted by factors outside itself; may even be so suppressed as to be invisible in the conduct and unsuspected in the wishes of the lover. Yet the desire to link their lives with the future is deeply woven into the love of all sound and healthy people who love supremely.

It is commonly said that most women marry for children, and not out of a personal love, and there is more truth in this saying than is good for the race. To-day, alas, many women cannot find the perfect and sensitive mate their hearts' desire and they hope in *any* marriage to get children which will mitigate the consequent loneliness of their lives. Sometimes they may, to some extent, succeed, but far less often than they imagine, for that strange and still but little understood force "heredity" steps in, and the son of the tolerated father may grow infinitely more like his physical father than he is like the dear delight his mother dreamed he might be.

Few girls have not pictured in day dreams the joy of holding in their arms their own beautiful babies. No man of their acquaintance, however, may seem fine enough to be their father. Until she has been crushed by experience, or, unless she listens with absolute belief to the depressing information of her elders, each girl believes that her own intense desire for perfection will be the principal factor in creating the beautiful babies of her dreams. Often it seems as though this power were granted, for women sometimes bear lovely children by fathers in whom one may seek in vain for any bodily grace or charm.

The century long working of economic laws based on physical force, the remnants of which still affect us, has resulted in man generally having the selective power and tending to choose for his wife the most beautiful or charming woman that his means allow; hence hitherto on the whole, the race has been bred from the better and more beautiful women. This has undoubtedly tended to keep the standard of physical form from sinking to the utter degradation which we see in the worst of the slums, and in institutions where live the feeble-minded offspring of inferior mothers who have wantonly borne children of fathers devoid of any realization of what they were doing.

From these avenues of shame and misery, however, I must steer my line of thought, for this book is written pre-eminently for the young, happy and physically well-conditioned pair who mating beautifully on all the planes of their existence, are living in married love.

Whether early in the days of their marriage or postponed for some months or more out of regard for his wife's body and beauty, the hour will come when the young husband yearning above her, sees in his wife's eyes the reflection of the future, and when their mutual longing springs up to initiate the chain of lives which shall repeat throughout the ages the bodily, mental and spiritual beauties of each other, which each holds so dear. Perhaps in lovers' talk and exquisite whispers they have spoken of this great deed on which they are embarking, and each has voiced that intense yearning which filled them to see another "with your eyes, your hair, your smile," living and radiant. The lovers dream that they will be repeated in others of their own creation, always young, running through the ages which culminate in the golden glories of the millennium.

The dream is so wonderful, the thought that it pictures in the mind so full of vernal beauty, light and vigour that, were facts commensurate with it, its result should spring all ready formed from between the lips of those who breathed its possibilities like Minerva from the head of Jove.

It seems incredible that such splendid dominant designs to fulfil God's purpose should be hindered, and made to bend and toil through the hard material facts of the molecular structure of the world, and that it is only many months afterwards that the first outward body is given to this dream, and that then it is in a form not strong and dancing in lightness and beauty but weak and helpless with many intensely physical necessities which for months and years will require the utmost fostering care or it will be destroyed by material effects, hostile and too strong for it. Yet such is the limitation of our powers of creation. And underneath the intense passion of love and all its rich dreams of beauty is the slow building, chemically molecule by molecule, biologically cell by cell, against obstacles the surmounting of which seems a superhuman feat.

Lovers who are parents give to each other the supremest material gift in the world, a material embodiment of celestial dreams which itself has the further power of vital creation.

In this and all my work, I speak to the normal, healthy and loving in an endeavour to help them to remain normal, healthy and loving, and thus to perfect their lives. So in this book I do not intend to deal with those whose marriages are mistaken ones, or with those who do not know true love. I write for those who having made a love match are passing together through the ensuing and surprising years, and incidentally doing one of the greatest pieces of work which human beings can do during their progress through this world, and that is creating the next generation.

In nature, the consummation of the physical act of union between lovers generally results in the conception of a new life. We share this physical aspect of mating and the resulting parenthood with most of the woodland creatures. How far many of the lowlier lives are conscious of the future results of their mating unions is a problem in elementary psychology beyond the realm of present knowledge. But that parenthood is the natural result of their union is to-day known, one must suppose, by almost all young couples who wed. I am still uncertain how far the two are *conscious* of this in the early days of their union, when every circumstance encourages that supreme self-centredness of happy youth. Much must depend on the age, and on the previous experience and education of the two; much also on their relative natures. A profoundly introspective and thoughtful man and woman are more liable than others to be speedily aware of the many interwoven strands of their joint lives, and to live consciously on several planes of existence simultaneously.

The supreme act of physical union as I have shown in my book, *Married Love,* consists fundamentally of three essential and widely differing reactions, having effects in correspondingly different regions. There is *(a)* the intimately personal effect on the internal secretions and general vitality of the individual partaking of that sacrament; *(b)* there is the social effect of the union of the two in a mutual act in which they must so perfectly blend and harmonize; and *(c)* there is the racial result which may lead to the procreation of a new life.

In the early days of the honeymoon, personal passion and the concentrated delight of each in the mate is probably more than sufficient in all its rich complexity to fill the consciousness of the two who are thus united in a life-long comradeship to form that highest unit, the pair. But as education and the conscious control of our lives grow, the young pair who are so blissfully self-centred as not to remember or not to be aware of the racial effects of their acts are probably decreasing in numbers. Among the best of those who marry to-day, the majority only enter upon parenthood or the possibility of parenthood when they feel justified in so doing. The young man who profoundly loves his wife and who considers the future benefit of their child, protects her from accidental conception or from becoming a mother at times when the strain upon her would be too great, or when he is unable to give her and the coming child the necessary care and support. That myriads of children are born without this consideration on the part of their parents applies to the commonalty of mankind, but not to the best.

Often to-day the betrothed young couple will speak openly and beautifully of the children they hope to have, while others equally full of the creative dream feel it too tender a subject to put into words, and may marry without ever having given expression to the possibility that they will generate through their love yet other lovers.

CHAPTER XV

Evolving Types of Women

> Deliverance is not for me in renunciation. I feel
> the embrace of freedom in a thousand bonds of
> delight.
> Thou ever pourest for me the fresh draught of thy
> wine of various colours and fragrance, filling this
> earthen vessel to the brim.
> No, I will never shut the doors of my senses. The
> delights of sight and hearing and touch will bear
> thy delight.
> Yes, all my illusions will burn into illumination
> or joy, and all my desires ripen into fruits of
> love.
>
> TAGORE: *Gitanjali.*

ONE of the great sources of disharmony in our social life is the extent of the extraordinary ignorance about ourselves which still persists. From this spring our conflicting opinions and diametrically opposed views, and also the apparently self-contradictory evidence on almost any point of fundamental importance which is brought before the public.

In no respect is there more conflict of opinion than concerning the age at which a woman should marry and become a mother. On the one hand, we have advocates of very early motherhood, and they point to the fact that a girl of seventeen is often already a woman and strongly sexed; they point to the hackneyed statement "that a girl matures sooner than a boy"; they point to the fine and healthy babies which very young mothers may bear and to the greater pliability and ease of birth, and these facts and their arguments may appear conclusive. On the other hand, the actual experience of many people conflicts with these apparently justified conclusions.

All the highly evolved races tend to prolong childhood and youth. All tend to replace early marriage by later marriage and parenthood to the obvious advantage of the race.

Marriage and parenthood at fourteen, fifteen and sixteen, which once were common in almost every country, are being replaced by later marriage and parenthood. As Finot 1913 says:—

A mystic chain appears to attach the age for love to the consideration enjoyed by women. In the Far East, woman is offered very young to the passion of man, and disappears from existence at the time her contemporaries are just beginning to live. Love, for this very reason, has a purely sensual stamp, degrading to man and to woman. The lengthening of the age of love elevates the dignity, and at the same time increases the longevity, of woman. Beyond the age of thirty or forty the woman, dead to love, was fit only for religion or witch-craft. Her life was shattered. Prematurely aged she went out of the living world. The prolonged summer of Saint-Martin in women will doubtless have consequences which we should be wrong to fear. There is a solidarity of ages. The cares bestowed on the child benefit the old man. The enlargement of the age of maturity allows the child longer to enjoy the years of life that are intended to form bodies and souls. . . The sentimental life of the country has undergone similar results. Balzac, in proclaiming the right to love on the part of the woman of thirty, aroused in his contemporaries astonishment bordering on indignation. In his day, was not a man of forty-four considered an old man? (Balzac: *Physiologie du Mariage)* Let us not forget that forty or fifty years before Balzac, a philosopher like Charles Fourier, despairing of the sentimental fate of young girls who had not found a husband before the age of . . . eighteen years, claimed for them the right to throw propriety to the winds. According to the author of the *Theorie des Quatre-Mouvement* (Charles Fourier, Leipzig, 1808), this was almost the critical age *(Problems of the Sexes,* transl. Jean Finot 1913).

The relative ages of husband and wife also have their influence, but should, to some extent, depend more on their *physiological* age than on their actual years. They should, however, not be widely different. As Saleeby says:—

The greater the seniority of the husband, the more widowhood will there be in a society. Every economic tendency, every demand for a higher standard of life, every aggravation for the struggle for existence, every increment of the burden of the defective-minded, tending to increase the man's age at marriage, which, on the whole, involves also increasing his seniority—contributes to the amount of widowhood in a nation.

We, therefore, see that, as might have been expected, this question of the age ratio in marriage, though first to be considered from the average point of view of the girl, has a far wider social significance. First, for herself, the greater her husband's seniority, the greater are her chances of widowhood, which is in any case the destiny of an enormous preponderance of married women. But further, the existence of widowhood is a fact of great social importance because it so often means unaided motherhood, and because, even when it does not, the abominable economic position of women in modern society bears hardly upon her. It is not necessary to pursue this subject further at the present time. But it is well to insist that this seniority of the husband has remoter consequences far too important to be so commonly overlooked *(Woman and Womanhood,* 1912).

I have observed many girls, who were in every true sense of the word girls (that is unconscious of personal sex feeling, still growing in bodily stature and still developing in internal organization) until they were nearly thirty years of age. In my opinion, the girl who is thoroughly well-balanced, with an active brain, a well-developed normally sexed body, natural artistic and social instincts is not more than a child at seventeen, and to marry her at that age or anything like it is to force her artificially, and to wither off her potentialities.

The type of woman who really counts in our modern civilization is, as a rule, not of age until she is nearly thirty. Not only does she *not* mature sooner than a boy; she matures actually later than a large number of men. I have now accumulated a wide and varied amount of evidence in favour of the view which I here propound, namely, that there is a most highly evolved type of woman in our midst. This type, which it will be agreed is the most valuable we possess, encompasses women of a wide range of potentialities; they have beautiful entirely feminine bodies, with all feminine and womanly instincts well developed, with a normal, indeed a rather strong, sex instinct and acute personal desires which tend to be concentrated on one man and one man alone. I will provisionally call this the late maturing type, for such a woman is generally incapable of real sex experience till she is about twenty-seven or thirty. I think that she is in line with the highest branch of our evolution, that she represents the present flower of human development, and that through her and her children the human race has the best hope of evolving on to still higher planes—but, and this is very important, she is not fitted for marriage until she is at least twenty-seven, probably later, her best child-bearing years may be after she is thirty-five, and her most brilliant and gifted children are likely to be born when she is about forty.

Personal evidence, and also facts in the interesting letters sent me by my readers have brought to my knowledge the existence of an important proportion of women who are absolutely unconscious of personal localized sex feeling until they are nearly or over thirty—one woman was nearly fifty before she felt and knew the real meaning of sex union though many years married.

From outward observation of the general physique of such of these women as I have seen face to face, I may say that, as a rule, they retain their youth long; they retain also a buoyancy and vitality which, if they are properly treated, and have the good fortune to be married at the right time to the right man, may remain with them almost throughout their lives. Such women not only prolong their girlhood, they defer their age. Such women have, of course, throughout the centuries appeared from time to time, and I fancy have generally in the past, and still often in the present, suffered acutely through marrying too young. When they marry too young they tend, by the forcing of their feelings, by the deadening through habit of their potentialities, by the trampling on the unfolded possibilities within them, to be turned artificially into a "cold type of woman."

Women now older tell me of the fact that for the first years of their married life they could give no response, but when they were respectively twenty-nine, thirty, thirty-one or more, they began first to feel they were truly women. Young husbands have written to me of their distress that their wives (aged about twenty to twenty-three), delightful girls in every respect, seemed utterly incapable of any response in the marital orgasm. Sometimes this depends on her conformation, but such an incapacity I often attribute to the girl's marriage being premature. When she is twenty-seven or twenty-eight perhaps her internal development will be complete, and she will then be ripe for the full enjoyment of marriage: but if instead of a considerate husband she marries one who merely uses her, she stands little chance ever of knowing the proper relation of wifehood and motherhood.

These facts which I could vary with details from individual experiences, in my opinion, indicate a profound truth in the development of the human race. It is this: not only do the higher races of human beings have a prolonged childhood and youth, but the most highly evolved, mentally, physically and racially, of our girls have not finished their potential growth into maturity until they are in the neighbourhood of thirty years of age.

Does this then mean that all marriage should be deferred till so late? By no means, nor is the above conclusion any reflection on the type of girl who ripens much more quickly. I fully recognize that from the point of view of their sex potentialities some girls are complete women at seventeen or eighteen, and that they may then be very strongly sexed indeed. Such women should marry young.

The marked differentiation of type of these very notably different women can be traced through many other aspects of their lives . . . It should be recognized that there are among us not only different races, but that in the same stock, sometimes in the same family of apparently no specially mixed ancestry, we may find one or more members of the late maturing, others of the early maturing type. Sometimes of two sisters, the elder may perhaps be still in mind a girl while her younger sister is a woman, as can be observed by anyone with a large circle of acquaintances. It would be well, I think, if humanity, whose proper study is mankind, were at least to know themselves sufficiently well to realize the existence of such different types, and their possible potential value as well as their differing needs. The energy at present wasted in the acrid statement of conflicting views would be so much better spent on the careful recording and recognizing of varying types.

The advice to marry young, which is in every respect socially wise and physiologically correct for some, should not be hurled indiscriminately at all women, because for the late maturing such advice is socially disadvantageous and physiologically wrong.

I am now ready to consider the question of the proper age for motherhood about which an immense variety of opinion is expressed. The general tendency has been, even in the last few years, to raise the age at which a girl may marry, and to raise the age which the medical profession advises as the earliest suitable for motherhood. But still one often hears of elders, whom one would in other respects like to follow, advising the early bearing of children.

Now I should like every potential parent to consider what type of child they want. Do they want to secure healthy, jolly little animals with no more brains than are sufficient to see them creditably through life? If so, let them have their children very early. Such healthy sound people with no special gifts are valuable, and there is much work in the world for them to do. On the other hand, do they want to take the risk for their child of a possibly less robust body, but with the possibility, indeed, in healthy families, almost the certainty, of an immensely greater brain power, and a more strongly developed temperament? Then let them have their children late. And if a man desires to have a child who may become one of the *master* minds whose discoveries, whose artistic creations, whose ruling power stamps itself upon the memory of our race, whose name is handed down the ages, then let the father who desires such a child mate himself with the long-young late-maturing type of woman I have just described, and let her bear that child sometime between the age of thirty-five and forty-five.

How often one hears some version of the phrase: "Yes, it is so sad, poor, dear Lord So-and-So, a charming man, but no brains at all ; his younger brother such a brilliant man; but that is always the way, the eldest sons in the aristocracy do seem to get the gift of property balanced by the lack of brains." Now I enquire, and I should like my readers to enquire, into the secret of this phenomenon, which is by no means universal, but is sufficiently common to be endorsed. In my opinion, the interpretation of this fact is that the earlier children were born when the mother was still too young to endow them with brains, particularly if the mother was one of the gifted and cultivated women of the late-maturing type.

This also leads me to consider another generality which is frequently used as an argument by those who oppose conscious and deliberate parenthood. Some people say that by the direct control of the size of the family to a small limited number which the parents definitely desire, we would be eliminating genius from our midst, and their argument runs: Look at Nelson, he was a fifth son; look at Sir Walter Scott, he was a third son; and so on. This to the uncritical seems conclusive, and many people of great capacity, ideals and heart, who otherwise would be wholly on my side in my claim that every child born shall be deliberately desired, and that all other conceptions shall be consciously prevented, are swayed by this argument and say: "Yes, your position would be obviously the right one for the race if it were not that later children are so often the better." I turn, therefore, to a consideration of the life histories of these men's mothers. Why was Nelson the genius of his family? Because his mother was too young to bear geniuses at the time she was bearing her elder children. But this is not yet a sufficiently accurate consideration of the subject; I want to know also of which type the mother was, for, in my opinion, the right age for the parenthood of a woman depends also on the type to which she belongs, whether the early maturing or the late maturing. If she knows herself to be the latter, after it is patent, as it must become patent to everyone once the idea is placed before them, that such women are in our midst, then that woman and her husband should usually defer parenthood until she has reached at least thirty years of age. If this were done, then not the fourth, fifth or seventh but the first child would stand a very great chance of being a world leader, a powerful mind, perhaps even a genius. First children have been geniuses (Sir Isaac Newton was an only child); all depends on the age, the conscious desire, the general type and the surrounding conditions during prenatal state of her infant, of the mother who bears him and the father from whom he also inherits potentialities.

A few investigations bearing on the effect of the parent's age have been published by the Eugenics Society and some individuals, but none of these appear to me to be of any value, for none take into account the necessary data concerning the type of the mother which I here point out, and in all the calculations crude errors occur.

The best woman, with comparatively *few* exceptions, is already and will still more in the future be the woman who, out of a long, healthy and vitally active life, is called upon to spend but a comparatively small proportion of her years in an *exclusive* subservience to motherhood.

A woman should have eighty to ninety active years of life; if she bears three or perhaps four children, she will, even if she gives up all her normal activities during the later months of pregnancy and the earlier of nursing, still have cut out of her life but a very small proportion of its total. She should, indeed, after she once is a mother, always devote a proportion of her energies to the necessary supervision of her children's growth and education, but with the increasing number of schools and specialists, nurses, teachers and instructors of all sorts, the individual mother has much less of the purely physical labour of her children than formerly. That this is not only so, but is *approved* by the State can be seen at once by imagining a working class mother insisting on keeping her child at home all day under her personal supervision— the School Inspector would step in and take the child from her for a certain number of hours every day. But this book is primarily for middle and upper class women, and for them motherhood increasingly should mean a *widening* of their interests and occupations.

The counter-idea still expressed, even by leading doctors and others, is that the whole capability of the individual mother should be devoted solely to contributing to her children. This is exemplified in the recent statement of Blair Bell: "A normal woman, therefore, would not exploit her capabilities for individual gain, but for the benefit of her descendants." This view is a false one and is based on a narrow vision.

This pictures an endless chain of fruitless lives all looking ever to some supreme future consummation which never materializes. By means of this perpetual sinking of woman's personality in a mistaken interpretation of her duty to the race, every generation is sacrificed in turn. The result has not been productive of good, happiness or beauty for the majority. No; the individual woman, normal or better than the average, *should* use her intellect for her individual gain in creative work; not only because of its value to the age and community in which she lives, but also for the inheritance she may thus give her children and so that when her children are grown up they may find in their mother not only the kind attendant of their youth, but their equal in achievement. With a woman of capacities perhaps still exceptional, but by no means so rare as some men writers would like to pretend, the pursuit of her work or profession and honourable achievement in it is not at all incompatible with but is highly beneficial to her motherhood. As Charlotte Gilman says:—

No, the maternal sacrifice theory will not bear examination. As a sex specialized to reproduction, giving up all personal activity, all honest independence, all useful and progressive economic service for her glorious consecration to the uses of maternity, the human female has little to show in the way of results which can justify her position. Neither by the enormous percentage of children lost by death nor the low average health of those who survive, neither physical nor mental progress, give any proof to race advantage from the maternal sacrifice. *—Women and Economics.*

CHAPTER XVII
Baby's Rights

> "The nation that first finds a practical reconciliation between science and idealism is likely to take the front place among the peoples of the world." DEAN INGE: *Outspoken Essays*

BABY's rights are fundamental. They are: To be wanted. To be loved before birth as well as after birth.

To be given a body untainted by any heritable disease, uncontaminated by any of the racial poisons.

To be fed on the food that nature supplies, or, if that fails, the very nearest substitute that can be discovered.

To have fresh air to breathe; to play in the sunshine with his limbs free in the air; to crawl about on sweet clean grass.

When he is good, to do what baby wants to do and not what his parents want; for instance, to sleep most of his time, not to sit up and crow in response to having his cheeks pinched or his sides tickled.

When he is naughty, to do what his parents want and not what he wants: to be made to understand the "law of the jungle." From his earliest days he must be disciplined in relation to the great physical facts of existence, to which he will always hereafter have to bow. The sooner he comprehends this, the better for his future.

Most young mothers, even those who have had the advantage of highly trained maternity nurses to assist them at first, later require authoritative advice about how to treat the baby for whom they have given so much, and to whom they wish to give every possible advantage. Many books give advice to the young mother and to these she may turn. I do not wish to duplicate what they say, but advise everyone who has an infant, even if they think they know all about the best method' of bringing it up, to possess a copy of Dr. Truby King's *Baby and How to Rear It* for reference. It is the most practical, sensible and best illustrated book of its kind.

There is, therefore, on the subject of baby's material rights not very much more that I need to say, but there is one elementary right very generally overlooked, and that is the right to love in anticipation.

Baby's right to be *wanted* is an individual right which is of racial importance. No human being should be brought into the world unless his parents desire to take on the responsibility of that new life which must, for so long, be dependent upon them.

Far too many of the present inhabitants of this earth who are *not* wanted because of their inferiority, were children who came to reluctant, perhaps horror-stricken, mothers. To this fact, I trace very largely the mental and physical aberrations which are to-day so prevalent; to this also I trace the bitterness, the unrest, the spirit of strife and malignity which seem to be without precedent in the world at present [see also *The Control of Parenthood,* final section, and, for the remedy, my book, *Wise Parenthood,* both published by Putnam].

The warped and destructive impulse of revolution which is sweeping over so many people at present must have its roots in some deep wrong.

Revolution is not a natural activity for human beings. Though the revolutionary impulse has swept through sections of humanity many times in its history, it is essentially unnatural, an indication of warping and poisoning, and a cause of further and perhaps irreparable damage.

Happy people do not indulge in revolution. Happy people with a deep sense of underlying contentment and satisfaction in life may yet strive ardently to improve and beautify everything round them. They strive in the same direction as the main current of life—that is the growth and unfolding of ever increasing beauty. The revolutionaries—bitter, soured and profoundly unhappy—pit their strength against the normal stream of life and destroy, break down and rob. Too long humanity has had to endure such outbreaks owing to its general blindness and lack of understanding of their causes.

Until the scientific spirit of profound inquiry into fundamental causes becomes general even in a small section of the community, superficial and apparently obvious explanations are accepted to account for results which really arise from profound and secret springs.

The "divine discontent" which has impelled humanity forward along the path of constructive progress is a very different thing from the bitter discontent which leads to revolutionary and destructive outbursts. The village blacksmith of the well-known song, using his healthy muscles on hard, useful work which gives him a deep physical satisfaction, may feel the former and help forward the stream of progress in his village.

The aim of reformers to-day should be to provide for every one neither ease nor comfort, nor high wages nor short hours, but the deeper necessities of a full and contented life, bodies able to respond with satisfaction to the strain of hard work performed under conditions which satisfy the mind in the most fundamental way of all—the deep, sub-conscious satisfaction which is given by the sweet smell of earth, by fresh air and sunshine, and green things around one.

We draw from all these things some subtle ingredient without which our natures are weakened so that a further strain sends them awry. To-day we are so deeply involved with the hydra-headed monster of the revolutionary spirit that there does not seem time to deal with it radically, to attempt to understand it, and consequently to conquer it forever. Even now, when for the first time humanity is on a large scale beginning to tackle fundamental problems, I have seen no indication that the source of revolution is being sought for in the right place.

What is the source of revolution?

The revolutionaries through the ages, feeling themselves jar with their surroundings, have been ensnared by the nearest obvious things, the happier surrounding of others. These they have endeavoured to snatch at and destroy, thinking thereby to improve their own and their comrades' lot. Their deductions, though profoundly false, have appeared even obviously right to many.

External grievances are what the revolutionary is out to avenge: external benefits are what he is out to gain. Generally this is expressed in terms of higher wages, a share, or all, of the capital of those supposed to be better off, or the material possessions of others. These are the things that nearly all strikers and revolutionaries are upsetting the world to get, thinking—perhaps sincerely—that these things will give them the happiness for which, consciously or unconsciously, they yearn. The truth is, however, that it is a much more intimate thing than money or possessions which they need. They need new bodies and new hearts.

Most of the revolutionaries I have met are people who have been warped or stunted in their own personal growth. One sees upon their minds or bodies the marks and scars of dwarfing, stunting or lack of balance. They have known wretchedness both in themselves and in their families far more intimate and penetrating than that of mere poverty.

That, they may answer, is an external grievance which has been imposed upon them by society. In effect they say: "Society has starved us, given us bad conditions." Thus they foster a grievance against "society" in their minds. One bitter leader said to me:—

I was one of fourteen children, and my mother had only a little three-roomed cottage near Glasgow. We nearly starved when I was young. I know what the poor suffer at the hands of society.

But it was not society that put fourteen children into that cottage; it was the mother herself. Her own ignorance, helpless ignorance perhaps, was the source of her children's misery. The most for which society can be blamed concerning that family is in tolerating such a plague-spot of ignorance in its midst. Nor is this pestilential ignorance by any means only confined to the financially poor.

This country, and nearly all the world, has innumerable homes in which the seed of revolution is sown in myriads of minds from the moment they are conceived. Revolted, horrorstricken mothers bear children whose coming birth they fear.

A starved, stunted outlook is stamped upon their brains and bodies in the most intimate manner before they come into the world, so oriented towards it that they must run counter to the healthy, happy constructive stream of human life.

What wonder at the rotten conditions of our population when these are common experiences of the mothers of our race:—

For fifteen years I was in a very poor state of health owing to continual pregnancy. As soon as I was over one trouble it was started all over again.[2]
Again :—

During pregnancy I suffered much. When at the end of ten years I determined that this state of things should not go on any longer.

Again :—

---

[2] I refer the reader to that poignant book, *Maternity, Letters from Working Women,* collected by the Women's Co-operative Guild. Bell, 1915.

My grandmother had twenty children. Only eight lived to about fourteen years; only two to a good old age.

Again :—

I cannot tell you all my sufferings during the time of motherhood. I thought, like hundreds of women to-day, that it was only natural, and that you had to bear it. I had three children and one miscarriage in three years.

Need I go on?

There lies the real root of revolution.

The secret revolt and bitterness which permeates every fibre of the unwillingly pregnant and suffering mothers has been finding its expression in the lives and deeds of their children. We have been breeding revolutionaries through the ages and at an increasing rate since the crowding into cities began, and women were forced to bear children beyond their strength and desires in increasingly unnatural conditions.

Also since women have heard rumours that such enslaved motherhood is not necessary, that the wise know a way of keeping their motherhood voluntary, the revolt in the mother has become conscious with consequent injury to the child.

Increasingly, the first of baby's rights is to be *wanted*.

Concerning baby's right to be fed on the food that nature supplies, or if that fails on the very nearest substitute that can be discovered, there are to-day so many who urge that an infant shall be fed by its own mother, that it is perhaps needless to repeat arguments so impressive. Nevertheless, perhaps it is as well to remind young mothers of two or three of the most vital facts. The first is that no artificial substitute, however perfectly prepared and chemically analysed, can possibly give those very subtle constituents which are found in the mother's own milk and which vary from individual to individual. These probably are in the nature of the vitamines now so well known in fresh food, but they are something more specifically individual than can be scientifically detected. The fresh milk of its own mother has a peculiar value to the child which is greater than that of any foster mother.

For this reason alone, were it the only one, every young mother should nurse her own baby if possible; but, on the other hand, to-day it not infrequently happens that the mother may have an apparent flow of milk, quite sufficient for the infant in quantity, but that milk may be devoid of the necessary supply of fat or sugars or some other ingredient for complete nutriment. When this is so, it is often wisest to allow the mother to nurse the child partly and to supplement its diet by other milk.

Various schools of doctors and maternity nurses have differed even on this matter, but it is quite obvious that if the actual food value of the mother's milk is below a certain point then the added value of its individual vitamine-like qualities will not wholly compensate for the loss of actual nourishment.

Among baby's rights, I should perhaps also make it clear that there is his right that he should not be used as a bulwark between his mother and another baby in a way which is sometimes recommended so that a mother may go on nursing her infant for a very long time, sometimes even into its second year, in the hope that this nursing may prevent her conceiving again. Such a course of action is very harmful both to the child and to her and should never be followed. Such a practice is, of course, much less common in this country (except among aliens) than it is abroad where I have seen healthy children of even three or four years of age nursing upon their mother's knees.

In these days, perhaps it is hardly necessary to accentuate baby's other rights since the century of the child dawned a generation ago. To-day it is perhaps almost more important to accentuate the rights of others who exist in the neighbourhood of a baby. But on the other hand if one looks penetratingly at the whole problem of character development, one sees that among baby's rights is its right to be trained from the very first so that its life shall be as little hindered by friction as may be possible: that it should be taught the elementary rules of conduct and necessary conformity with the hard material facts of existence from the very first. A wise nurse's or mother's training from the earliest weeks of infancy may make or mar a future man's or woman's chance of getting on in the world and making a success of their lives, by making or marring the character, the capacity to obey, the formation of regular and hygienic habits and the realization of the physical facts of the world.

The ancient Greeks taught their youth to reverence that which was beneath them, that which was around them, and that which was above them. In my opinion this right of youth to be placed in its proper orientation in relation to the world has been neglected of late. We are suffering from the wayward revolt from an earlier and perhaps harsher type of mistake, that of too greatly controlling and thwarting the child's impulses. We must maintain a just balance and return to the due mean in which the right of a child, not only to be well born but well trained, is universally recognized.

CHAPTER XIX

The Cost of Coffins

He only is free who can control himself.   EPICTETUS.

The imposition of motherhood upon a married woman in absolute despite of her health and of the interests of the children is none the less an iniquity because it has at present the approval of Church and State.
SALEEBY: *Woman and Womanhood.*

WHY do poor slum mothers buy more coffins than do the same number of rich women? The incredulous may answer this question by asserting that they don't, but as a matter of fact they do. The Registrar-General's Report for 1911 shows that of every thousand births in the upper and middle classes, 76.4 babies die, while of a thousand births in the homes of unskilled workmen (this would be the class of the "poor" mothers) 152.5 babies die.

So that it is clear that if each member of this poorest class of mothers had exactly the same number of babies as each mother of the rich class, she would have to purchase about two coffins for every coffin bought by those whose babies are not so prone to die.

There is, however, another fact which completes the proof of my first sentence. The upper and middle classes do not have so many children per family as do the poorest class. To a thousand married people in the upper and middle classes there were born in 1911 119 babies, but to the poor mothers—the wives of the unskilled workmen—there were born 213. So that in addition to buying twice as many coffins per thousand children born, these poor mothers have nearly twice as many coffins again, owing to the fact that nearly twice as many children are born to them.

I wonder if poor women have ever asked themselves if they can afford coffins at this rate?

Of course the coffins of these poor little babies are very small, and do not require very much wood to make them. But let us think in what other ways they cost: To the mother they cost not only all the little the baby had eaten, and used in the way of clothes before its death, but all the wastage of her own vitality while she was bearing it; she could not work so well, at any rate towards the end of the time. Home duties had to be somewhat neglected; the older children had to go to school dirtier and less cared for; the husband had less comfort and fewer smiles; everyone in the family was poorer, not only in material things and in the work that might make material things, but in happiness and buoyancy.

It needs no imagination to realize, when you have once grasped these facts, that poor people are much less able to spare the cost of a doomed baby than are the better class people. Then why do they so often indulge in this tragic luxury? Chiefly through lack of knowledge, through ignorance, particularly on the part of the mother.

Often ignorance is blind and unaware that it is ignorance, stupidly blundering through life; but this is not always the mother's attitude. She may, indeed she often does, passionately desire knowledge and seek for it wherever she thinks she may find it in her restricted circle. Too tragically often she is baffled in her search.

Some years before the war, when I was lecturing at a Northern University, a little incident opened my eyes to this fact. I was young and had not encountered this aspect of life before, and it burnt itself into my consciousness as one of the most vivid impressions of my life. It was this:—

One of my students was a woman who was hoping to qualify as a medical doctor, and she was having tea with me and chatting about the events of the day. As part of her training she had been assisting the doctor in dealing with out-patients at a hospital, and a woman had brought in a miserable little baby, which wailed all the time and which the mother explained wouldn't put on any flesh or grow into a nice, healthy baby whatever she did with it.

The mother, with tears in her eyes, made an intensely earnest appeal to the doctor to tell her what was to her unaccountably wrong with the infant.

She was a fine strapping woman, and thought her babies ought to be large and healthy. She said this was her third or fourth, and the others had all died when they were very little.

This happened more than seven years ago. Thank God our racial attitude has changed since then.

The doctor put her off with some soothing platitudes, but the woman driven to despair said: "I believe there's something wrong with my man. If there's something wrong with my man I won't have babies no more—it's just cruel to see them miserable like this and have them dying one after the other. Won't you, for God's sake, tell me whether there's anything wrong with my man or not?" This appeal was met by the assurance that there was nothing wrong, and she should go on having babies and do her duty by her husband.

My medical woman student said that it was glaringly obvious that the baby was syphilitic.

I asked her why she did not immediately tell the mother the truth. She shrugged her shoulders and said: "I've got my exam to pass; if I did a thing like that Dr. —— would stop me going to the hospital. I can't afford to take risks like that. Why, he might not only stop me, but it would do the other women students a lot of harm too."

This was before the war, and England was less enlightened, less eager for medical women's assistance than the war has made her, and it was then a fight for a girl to get a footing in the hospitals for the wide experience she needed for a general practice.

I vowed to myself that I would never forget that mother, and that some day I would batter at the brazen gates of knowledge on her behalf.

Here was a mother with a glimmering of the truth, seeking passionately for knowledge from the one person she had a right to turn to for this knowledge, and she was put off with lies, encouraged again to bear the cost of a hopelessly doomed birth; to risk the agonies of child-birth, to bring into the world a creature who for a short spell would be tormented and then would cost her a coffin.

By refusing his scientific advice, that doctor in reality sent that woman, whose desire to know was stirred, to the gossip of the slum alley and the street corner. There she would get a blurred and inaccurate, if not actually harmful, idea of what he should have been able to tell her in a clean, simple language based on scientific fact.

When this is put down on paper, I feel as though it would be ridiculous to begin to point out the monstrous cruelty and the monstrous folly of such an action as that doctor's. Yet such action was not isolated, it did not depend on one man's warped conceptions of loyalty to another unknown man, "the husband." Since the war a public realization of the racial destructiveness of such diseases has been increased and the woman and her husband would to-day be more likely to receive medical treatment.

But even to-day if a mother is truly told that there is "something wrong with her man," would she also certainly be told how in wise and healthy fashion she can herself supplement what his criminal negligence neglected? If a husband is careless and callous a woman must save herself and the community from the waste and the misery of irretrievably doomed births.

She will indeed be an exceptionally lucky woman if she to-day finds in public hospitals doctors to whom she could turn for knowledge how *best* to control conception, though such knowledge is not only essential to her private well-being, but essential to her in the fulfillment of her duties as a citizen.

This little incident is but one illustration of many aspects of the subject. It is not only *disease* which necessitates restraint on parenthood. No healthy woman can bear a long series of infants in rapid succession without loss both to them and to herself. This is discussed in my *Wise Parenthood.*

Anyone who thinks will see clearly that no civilized country, not even the richest in the world, can afford babies' coffins. Though they are smaller than grown-up people's they are more costly, for they are waste and nothing but waste. A grown-up individual, man or woman, has, we hope at any rate, given some return to the community in work or in ideas for all that his life has cost. But the infant's death is sheer unmitigated waste.

If all the mothers who realize this and who feel their need for the best help that science can give them, would insist and persist in their enquiries for a knowledge of the most reliable results of modern science, they would in the end succeed in getting them. There is enough knowledge now in the world for the race to transform itself in a couple of generations.

CHAPTER XX

The Creation of a New and Irradiated Race

Ah, Love! could thou and I with fate
conspire
To grasp this sorry Scheme of Things
entire,
Would not we shatter it to bits—and then
Remould it nearer to the Heart's desire.
            OMAR KHAYYAM.

ON parents' love for the helpless child depends the existence of our race. Human parenthood necessitates not only the desire for offspring, but the willing care of them during the long years while they are helpless and dependent. Were this desire and willingness not deeply implanted in us our race would become extinct, as in some strange way, the higher type of ancient Greeks vanished from the world.

Not only throughout the lower creatures do we find the responsibilities of parenthood increasing as we go up the scale towards the higher, but, even in the various grades of highly civilized man, the responsibility for the children is ever greater in proportion with the general culture and position of the parents.

Not many years ago the labourer's child could be set to work early and could very shortly earn his keep; while at the same time the young gentleman was an expense and care to his father and mother until he had passed through the University of Oxford or Cambridge, and amongst some even until he had made his "finishing" world tour. The trend of legislation has continuously extended the age of irresponsible youth in the lower and lower middle classes, until it now approaches that of the middle and upper class youth. A stride in this direction was taken by the last Education Act, which has made education compulsory throughout the whole country to an age which is nearly university age.

I need not labour the resulting effect of the ever increasing prolongation of youth. It is not only apparent but has received sufficient treatment from the hands of various authors and thinkers.

Its corollary, however, has still not received that clear and direct thought which its significance demands. Parenthood under the present *regime,* is not only an increasing responsibility and expense, it has become so great a strain upon the resources of those who have for themselves and their children a high standard of living that it is tending to become a rare privilege for some who would otherwise gladly propagate large families.

As Dean Inge reminded us *(Outspoken Essays,* 1919), there was a stage in the high civilization of Greece when slaves were only allowed to rear a child as a reward for their good behaviour. I find a curious parallel to this in the treatment of a section of our society by our present community.

Crushed by the burden of taxation which they have not the resources to meet and to provide for children also: crushed by the national cost of the too numerous children of those who do not contribute to the public funds by taxation, yet who recklessly bring forth from an inferior stock individuals who are not self-supporting, the middle and superior artisan classes have, without perceiving it, come almost to take the position of that ancient slave population. It is only as a reward for their thrift and foresight, for their care and self-denial that they find themselves able (that is allowed by financial circumstances) to have one or perhaps two children. Hence by a strange parallel working of divers forces, the best, the thriftiest, the most serious-minded, the most desiring of parenthood are to-day those who are forced by circumstances into the position of the ancient slave and allowed to rear but one or two children as a result perhaps of a lifetime of valuable service and of loving union with a wife well fitted to bear more offspring. While on the other hand, society allows the diseased, the racially negligent, the thriftless, the careless, the feebleminded, the very lowest and worst members of the community, to produce innumerable tens of thousands of stunted, warped, and inferior infants. If they live, a large proportion of these are doomed from their very physical inheritance to be at the best but partly self-supporting, and thus to drain the resources of those classes above them which have a sense of responsibility. The better classes, freed from the cost of the institutions, hospitals, prisons and so on, principally filled by the inferior stock, would be able to afford to enlarge their own families, and at the same time not only to save misery but to multiply a hundredfold the contribution in human life-value to the riches of the State.

The immensity of the power of parenthood, both on the personal lives which it brings into existence, and on the community of which each individual is to form a part, is not yet perceived by our Statesmen in its true perspective.

The power of parenthood ought no longer to be exercised by all, however inferior, as an "individual right." It is profoundly a duty and a privilege, and it is essentially the concern of the whole community. It should be the policy of the community to encourage in every way the parenthood of those whose circumstances and conditions are such that there is a reasonable anticipation that they will give rise to healthy, well-endowed future citizens. It should be the policy of the community to discourage from parenthood all whose circumstances are such as would make probable the introduction of weakened, diseased or debased future citizens. It is the urgent duty of the community to make parenthood impossible for those whose mental and physical conditions are such that there is well-nigh a certainty that their offspring must be physically and mentally tainted, if not utterly permeated by disease. That the community should allow syphilitic parents to bring forth a sequence of blind syphilitic infants is a state of affairs so monstrous that it would be hardly credible were it not a fact.

Parenthood, with the divine gift of love in its power, with the glorious potentialities of handing on a radiant, wholesome, beautiful youth should be a sacred and preserved gift, a privilege only to be exercised by those who rationally comprehend the counter-balancing duties. But so long as parenthood is kept outside the realm of rational thought and reasoned action, so long will we as a race slide at an ever-increasing speed towards the utter deterioration of our stock through the reckless increase of the debased, which is necessarily counterbalanced by the unnatural limiting of the families of the more educated and responsible, whose sense of duty to the unborn forbids them to bring into the world children whom they cannot educate and environ at least as well as they themselves were reared.

In earlier generations the child was taught to speak of its parents in a respectful and grateful tone as the "august authors of its being," but this right and proper instruction in reverence was coupled with an arbitrary disposal of the child, and a certain harshness in its training against which the later generations have revolted. As is usual the reformers have deviated from rectitude in the opposite direction, so that today to find children with deep respect for their parents is uncommon. Reverence is being exacted by some rather from the parent towards the child as a fresh, new and unspoilt being. This too often results in spoiling the child, which is an equally foolish and hampering proceeding. The child should be taught from its earliest days profound respect, reverence and gratitude towards its parents, and in particular towards its mother, for of her very life she gave it the incomparable gift of life. True parents give the child the best and freshest and most beautiful impulses of their lives, and, at the cost of bodily anguish the mother bears it, and its parents for long years nurture it, sacrificing many enjoyments which they might have but for the cost and care of rearing it. This should be realized by the child, who then cannot but feel gratitude to and reverence for the authors of its being.

The sheer beauty of the world, were there no other gain from living, is so great that the gift of eyes and a mind to perceive it should place the recipient of that gift for ever in a reverential debt towards the pair who gave.

But the value of the beauty of life, and a just appreciation of the immense gift which parenthood confers cannot be realized by all. To-day alas, millions are born into circumstances so wretched that life can scarcely involve a perception of beauty, or a probability of moral action and social service. Also many myriads of children are born of parents to whom they can feel that they owe nothing, because they know or inwardly perceive that they were not desired, that they were not profoundly and nobly loved throughout their coming, that they were hurled into this existence through accident, self-indulgence or stupidity. Yet parenthood which grants life even on these terms is a wonderful power, a cruel and relentless force perverted from its divine possibilities.

Youth tends ever to right itself if it but escape the taint of the profound racial diseases, and the gift of a well-conditioned body is the creation of an incomparable set of co-ordinated powers in a world in which the potentialities for the use of those powers is magical.

Innumerable are the efforts at present being made by countless different societies, official bodies and individual reformers to diminish the ever increasing ill-health and deterioration of our race, but their efforts are a fight on the losing side unless the fundamental and hitherto uncontrollable factors which make for health are there.

Doctors may cure every disease known to humanity, but while they are so doing, fresh diseases, further modifications of destructive germs, may spring into existence, the possibility of which has recently been demonstrated by French scientists who have experimented on the rapid changes which may be induced in "germs."

Prisons and reformatories, municipal milk, the feeding of school children, improvement in housing, reform of our marriage laws, schools for mothers, even schools for fathers, garden cities—not all these useful and necessary things together and many more added to them will ever touch the really profound sources of our race, will ever cause freedom from degeneracy and ill-health, will ever create that fine, glorious and beautiful race of men and women which hovers in the dreams of our reformers. Is then this dream out of reach and impossible; are then all our efforts wasted? No, the dream is not impossible of fulfilment; but, at present, our efforts are almost entirely wasted because *they are built upon the shifting sand and not upon the steady rock.*

The reform, *the one central reform,* which will make all the others of avail and make their work successful *is the endowing of motherhood, not with money but with the knowledge of her own power.*

For the power of a mother, consciously exerted in the voluntary procreation and joyous bearing of her children is the greatest power in the world. It is through its conscious and deliberate exercise, and through that alone, that the race may step from its present entanglements on to a higher plane, where bodies will be not only a delight to their possessors, but efficient tools in the service of the souls which temporarily inhabit them.

I maintain that this wonderful rejuvenescence and reform of the race need not be a dim and distant dream of the future. It is hovering so close at hand that it is actually within reach of those who to-day are in their young maturity; we, at present in the flesh may link hands with grandchildren belonging to a generation so wonderful, so endowed, and so improved out of recognition that the miseries and the depravity of human nature, to-day so wide-spread, may appear like a black and hideous memory of the past, as incredible to them as the habits of cannibals are to us.

An ideal too distant, too remote, may interest the dreamer and the reformer possibly, but it cannot inspire a whole nation. An ideal within the range of possibility, that each one of us who lives a full lifetime may actually perceive, such an ideal can spur and fire the imagination, not only of our own nation, but of the world. It is my prayer that I may present such a racial ideal, not only to my own people but to humanity. It is my prayer that I may live to see in the generation of my grandchildren a humanity from which almost all the most blackening and distressing elements have been eliminated, and in which the vernal bodily beauty and unsullied spiritual power of those then growing up will surpass anything that we know to-day except among the rare and gifted few. This is not a wild dream; it is a real potentiality almost within reach. The materialization of this vital racial vision is in the hands of the mothers for the next twenty or thirty years.

If every woman will but consciously and deliberately exercise the powers of her motherhood after learning of those powers; if she bear only those children which she and her mate ardently desire; if she refuse to bear any but these, and if she so space these children that she herself rests and recovers vitality between their births, and during their coming she lives in such a way as I have indicated in the preceding chapters, and if at the same time the deadly and horrible scourges of the venereal diseases and the multitude of ramifications of racial baseness are eliminated *as they can be,* then with a comparatively small percentage of accidents and unforeseeable errors, the quality of those born will enormously improve, and by a second generation all should be already far on the highway to new and wonderful powers, which are to-day almost unsuspected.

What are the greatest dangers which jeopardize the materialization of this glorious dream of a human stock represented only by well-formed, desired, well-endowed beautiful men and women? Two main dangers are in the way of its consummation; the first is ignorance. It is difficult to reach the untutored mind, to teach a public hardened and deadened to callousness and the lack of dreams of their own; even though if one could but reach them it would be possible to make them understand.

A second and almost greater danger is not a simple ignorance, but the inborn incapacity which lies in the vast and ever increasing stock of degenerate, feeble-minded and unbalanced who are now in our midst and who devastate social customs. These populate most rapidly, these tend proportionately to increase, and these are like the parasite upon the healthy tree sapping its vitality. These produce less than they consume and are able only to flourish and re-produce so long as the healthier produce food for them; but by ever weakening the human stock, in the end they will succumb with the fine structure which they have destroyed.

There appear then two obstacles which might block the materialization of my racial vision; on the one hand the ignorance of those who have latent powers. This only needs to be stirred by knowledge and the inspiration of an ideal, to become potent. This obstacle is not unsurmountable. If one but speaks in sufficiently burning words, if one but writes sufficiently contagiously, the ideas must spread with ever increasing acceleration. Ignorance must be vanquished by winged knowledge. I hold it to be the duty of the dreamer of great dreams not only to express them in such a way that cognate souls may also perceive them. It is the duty of a seer to embody his message in such a form that its beauty is apparent and the vision can be seen by all the people. The infectiousness of disease, the contagion of destructive and horrible bacterial germs have become a commonplace in our social consciousness, and we have forgotten, and our artists have in recent years tended ever more and more to forget that the highest form of art should also be infectious. Goodness, beauty and prophetic vision have as strong a contagious quality as disease if they are embodied in a form rendered vital by the mating of truth and beauty.

To overcome mere ignorance in others is, therefore, by no means a hopeless task, and it is the valiant work of the artist-prophet. Youth is the time to catch the contagion of goodness. To youth I appeal.

The other obstacle presents a deeper and more difficult task. It must deal with the terrible debasing power of the inferior, the depraved and feeble-minded, to whom reason means nothing and can mean nothing, who are thriftless, unmanageable and appallingly prolific. Yet if the good in our race is not to be swamped and destroyed by the debased as the fine tree by the parasite, this prolific depravity must be curbed. How shall this be done? A very few quite simple Acts of Parliament could deal with it.

Three short and concise Bills would be sufficient to afford the most urgent social service for the preservation of our race. They should be simply worded and based on possibilities well within the grasp of modern science.

The idea of sterilization has not yet been very generally understood or accepted, although it is an idea which our civilization urgently needs to assimilate. I think that a large part of the objections to it, often made passionately and eloquently by those from whom one would otherwise have expected a more intelligent attitude, is due to complete ignorance of the facts. Even otherwise instructed persons confuse sterilization with castration. The arguments which to-day in a chance discussion of the subject are always brought forward against sterilization have been, in my experience, only those which apply to castration. To castrate any male is, of course, not only to deprive him of his manhood and thus to injure his personal consciousness, but to remove bodily organs, the loss of which adversely affects his mentality and which will also affect the internal secretions which have a profound influence on his whole organization. I fully endorse the views of the opponents of this process.

It is, however, neither necessary to castrate nor is it suggested by those who, like myself, would like to see the sterilization of those totally unfit for parenthood made an immediate possibility, indeed made compulsory. As Dr. Havelock Ellis stated in an article in the *Eugenics Review,* Vol. I, No. 3, October 1909, pp. 203-206, sterilization under proper conditions is a very different and much simpler matter and one which has no deleterious and far reaching effects on the whole system. The operation is trivial, scarcely painful, and does not debar the subject from experiencing all his normal reaction in ordinary union; it only prevents the procreation of children.

It has been found in some States of America, and as I know from private correspondents in this country, there are men who would welcome the relief from the ever present anxiety of potential parenthood which they know full well would be ruinous to the future generation.

There is also the possibility of sterilization by the direct action of "X" rays. At present sterility is known as an unfortunate danger to those engaged in scientific research with radium, but it might, under control, be wisely used as a painless method of sterilization. This may prove of particular value for women in whom the operation corresponding to the severance of the ducts of the man is more serious. It appears however, not always to be permanent in its effect: In some circumstances this may be an advantage, in others a disadvantage.

With reference to the sterilizing effect of "X"-rays, the following quotation from F. H. Marshall, *The Physiology of Reproduction,* 1910, is pertinent:—

A more special cause of sterility in men is one which operates in the case of workers with radium or the Röntgen rays. Several years ago Albers-Schönberg noticed that the X-rays induced sterility in guinea pigs and rabbits, but without interfering with the sexual potency. These observations have been confirmed by other investigators, who have shown, further, that the azoöspermia is due to the degeneration of the cells lining the seminal canals. In men it has been proved that mere presence in an X-ray atmosphere incidental to radiography sooner or later causes a condition of complete sterility, but without any apparent diminution of sexual potency. As Gordon observes, for those working in an X-ray atmosphere adequate protection for all parts of the body not directly exposed for examination or treatment is indispensable, but, on the other hand, the X-rays afford a convenient, painless and harmless method of inducing sterility, in cases in which it is desirable to effect this result.

When Bills are passed to ensure the sterility of the hopelessly rotten and racially diseased, and to provide for the education of the childbearing woman so that she spaces her children healthily, our race will rapidly quell the stream of depraved, hopeless and wretched lives which are at present ever increasing in proportion in our midst. Before this stream at present the thoughtful shrink but do nothing. Such action as will be possible when these bills are passed will not only increase the relative *proportion* of the sound and healthy among us who may consciously contribute to the higher and more beautiful forms of the human race, but by the elimination of wasteful lives which are to-day seldom self-supporting, and which are so largely the cause of the cost and outlay of public money in their institutional treatment and their partial relief, will check an increasing drain on our national resources. The setting free of this public money would make it possible for those now too heavily taxed to reproduce their own and more valuable kinds.

The miserable, the degenerate, the utterly wretched in body and mind, who when reproducing multiply the misery and evil of the world, would be the first to be thankful for the escape such legislation would offer from the wretchedness entailed not only on their offspring but on themselves. The Labour Party, all Progressives, and all Conservatives who desire to conserve the good can unite to support measures so directly calculated to improve the physical condition, the mental happiness and the general well-being of the human race.

Even to-day almost all the thriftiest and better of the working class, and the artisan class in particular, are already in the ranks of those who are sponged upon, and to some extent taxed, for the upkeep of the incompetent, and it is just from among the best artisan and from the middle class that the most serious minded parents and those who recognize their racial responsibilities are principally to be found. There is throughout the whole Labour movement, as throughout the less vocal but deeper feeling of the middle class, a passionate desire to eliminate the misery and human degradation which on every hand to-day saddens the tender conscience. The limiting of their own families to meet the pressure of circumstances will never achieve their desires. The best to-day are making less and less headway, and the inferior are increasing more and more in proportion to them.

Directly, however, the need for such legislation as I have outlined above is realized, and such legislation is passed, then the tide will be turned. Then, at last, we shall begin to see the elimination of the horror and degradation of humanity, which at present is apparently so hopeless and permanent a blot upon the world. And then, and then at once, will the positive effects of the conscious working of love and beauty and desired motherhood begin to take effect. The evolution of humanity will take a leap forward when we have around us only fine and beautiful young people, all of whom have been conceived, carried and born in true homes by conscious, powerful and voluntary mothers.

Meanwhile the prison reformers, psychoanalysts, doctors, teachers and reformers of all sorts will be going on with their reforms, and will be claiming this and that wonderful improvement in the school children, and they will probably never realize that it will not be their reforms which have worked these apparent miracles; it will be the change in the attitude of the mother, the return to the position of power of the mother, her voluntary motherhood, the conscious and deliberate creation by the mother and her mate of the fine and splendid race which to-day, as God's prophet, I see in a vision and which might so speedily be materialized on earth.

A New Gospel
To All Peoples
(1920)

A Revelation of God Uniting
Physiology and the Religions of Man

First Delivered to the Bishops in Session at
Lambeth 1920

THROUGH

Marie Carmichael Stopes

PREFATORY NOTE

SEVERAL of those who have read the following words have inquired about their inception. It is due, therefore, to the reader to make a short explanation.

While it is a fundamental tenet of the Christian Religion that the devout soul should be in a direct relation with God, yet it is strange that when this is true, astonishment and incredulity, rather than acceptance based on confirmatory experience, is usual. There is also a curious and all too prevalent idea that the study of abstruse science, and in particular science which involves biological research, generates in an individual an incapacity for true religious experience, if not an actual scepticism concerning its reality. The existence of both such concepts is so prevalent that it may cause surprise to many that I, a trained and technical scientist, have a message for the world clothed in a form characteristic of religious experience. No explanation will satisfy the confirmed sceptic. Yet it may perhaps reassure those who incline towards a religious attitude of mind, although perhaps not adhering to any religious sect, to be told that I can see no cause for inner conflict in a person possessing both an intellect skilled in the technicalities of modern science and a heart in tune with that higher and inspiring influence which all the earth's peoples commonly call God.

The way in which the following words were written is exactly as follows: During the last week of June 1920 I was, like most other members of the reading public, aware of the proposed Conference of the Anglican Bishops at Lambeth; I was not, however, intending to communicate with them. That week it chanced that I spent an afternoon alone in the cool shades of the old yew woods on the hills behind my home: While penetrated by that calm beauty there came, suddenly and quite explicitly, exact instructions in the words which follow. I was told: "Say to my Bishops"—what is found in these pages. At the conclusion of the message I arose and went home instantly; sent for my secretary; and there and then, without going into the house, redictated to him what had been dictated to me. The message was then printed as quickly as could be arranged and a copy sent to each of the Bishops at the Conference.

It may be asked what place a Prophet can have in the modern world of thought, for in these days our knowledge of the laws of Nature and of new truths is derived by scientific experiment or the observations of minute structure revealed by the microscope; it may be urged that while in the ancient days man's knowledge of truth depended on the inspiration of the Prophets, it is so no longer. To this the answer is as follows: To-day, through the discoveries of individual scientists, we have available a vast number of new facts and truths which lie like piles of loose sand grains, incoherent and unabsorbed by the spirit of our people. These grains of truth are scattered as, sometimes irritating, fragments not yet interwoven with our *feelings,* our social consciousness, our ethical and religious codes. The work of a Prophet now is to select and transmute the truths given to the world through scientific discovery and weld them into our religious and social consciousness. The modern Prophet, therefore, must have a wide acquaintance with scientific discovery; added to which, for the accomplishment of this transmutation, direct inspiration is required to-day as much as it was ever required in the dim ages of the past when man's paths of access to truth were fewer.

When sending the gospel which follows to the Bishops I felt that conventional members of the English Church were less likely sincerely to believe that God does still communicate with His individual servants (though it is one of the fundamental tenets of their faith) than were many who are reputed to be less religious. The Bishops having dispersed without satisfying the yearnings of those who desired help in the most intricate and intimate of social needs, the message can no longer be left in Episcopal hands. It was naturally given first to the Anglican Bishops because my body, my home, and my language are English; but the Message is to all peoples of all religions, Buddhists, Mahomedans, Jews, Gentiles, Greeks, and all others. All worship the One God, and from Him came these truths.

Whoever may receive it, the publication to all peoples of this gospel is neither my choice nor my design, but my explicit and God-given duty. If any words in it fail to convince it must be that they are wrongly transcribed, which would be due to my faulty memory in the moments which passed between its transmission to me and my re-dictation.

MARIE C. STOPES

GIVONS GROVE,
LEATHERHEAD.

A NEW GOSPEL

TO ALL PEOPLES

First delivered to the Anglican Bishops assembled at Lambeth, 1920

[My Lords,
 I speak to you in the name of God. You are His Priests. I am His Prophet.
 I speak to you of the mysteries of the union of man and woman.]

OF the highest union of the perfectly loving man and woman the Church has not hitherto had the full revelation of God, for this has only been made possible in these later days through the revelation of His truths which have been won by Science. The requirements of human life have changed with the fulfilment of the years. Devout hearts may receive to-day truths which human experience was not ripe to perceive when Christ gave His messages to His disciples. There are revelations of meaning and wisdom in one generation which the fulfilment of time may render meaningless or destructive to another generation. God's Ministers of the Church have known some facets of this truth; hence, of the rules laid down by Levitical Law they select for Christian observance but a part. Of further revelations of this truth I would now speak.

From the hidden mysteries of creation Science has made known many truths, which, as there is but one Truth, should be built into the edifice of human conduct in God's service. In the dim past human knowledge and religion were as upon the two slopes of a pyramid. At the base, far distant from, and out of sight of each other, they had no sign that they were related, but towards the apex they approach; and now, in these recent days, those upon the slope of Science may look over and clasp the hands of those upon the slope of Religion.

Concerning the conduct of the body, that variously beautiful instrument of the soul, revelation has been delayed. And, lacking direct instruction on divers most complex difficulties, the Priests of God have led the people perforce much as a blind man leadeth the blind, feeling for old landmarks and tracks worn by the feet of those gone before. To-day God sends a new revelation and a new Gospel. Hearken unto it.

Harden not your hearts against the voice of God's revelation given in this present time. Say not among yourselves that God hath no more a living Prophet, and that nineteen centuries ago God spoke to humanity for the last time. As the needs of the people grow and change with their growth new revelations are given to throw light upon the footsteps of our human race toward the heavenly perfection of beauty. Say not among yourselves that if Christ did not speak of the perplexities which are to-day in the hearts of the multitude that He intended that these perplexities should be left over for ever unresolved. Say not among yourselves that Paul His Prophet, who saw Him nineteen hundred years ago, received from Him the final revelation for humanity upon the greatest of all vital mysteries. The vivifying beauty of the love of mates is for ever growing upwards.

Paul spoke with Christ nineteen hundred years ago. God spoke with me to-day. For nineteen centuries the reverent heart and brain of man have searched the mysteries of creation and piece by piece have won fragments of the new laws of life. Laws dreamed of within their hearts by the beloved of God dimly through all the centuries shall now be known and revealed in the light of knowledge and accepted by the minds and hearts of all, open in the clarity of essential truth.

The first of these mysteries is that God in the beginning not only created mankind male and female, but that, when the two are united, in the intangible but inviolable bonds of love, they are ONE, and thus form a more complex and perfected PERSON, a higher unit than can be presented in any other way upon this earth. The second of these mysteries is that the two in their acts of union enrich and vitalise each other, each adding mutually to the other's proper powers. When with rectitude the two bodily unite in obedience to the laws evidently ordained and clearly set forth by the physiological rhythms, by the daily, monthly, and yearly pulsations of the body, they transfer each to each not only the vitalising wave of love, but in their bodies each receives from each substances materially presented as chemical and ultra-chemical molecules. The interchange of these between man and woman is slow: hence hastiness and one-sided passion in the act are violations of the sacred union, and are to be condemned.

As the chemical molecules of bread and water are fraught with vitalizing properties when slowly ingested into the bodily system, and may be transmuted into human creative vitality in the form of human work or achievement, so the chemical molecules together with their still subtler concomitants, which man and woman mutually throw off and mutually receive only in the completest union of sex, enrich and vitalise the nature of each and may be transmuted into forms of human energy not otherwise to be produced.

God through Science reveals that without due balance of the subtle internal secretions of the sacred organs of sex neither child, nor unmated man nor woman, can be whole individuals, and this is true of him who most determinedly maintains an absolute celibacy. The life-long influence of sex is no chance happening. God through Science now reveals that by the due mingling of the subtle secretions released when a man and woman are truly united a further enrichment is given, and the pair become as the years pass more than any dissevered and unmated units can ever be: they become the highest expression of human life on earth.

Each member of the pair gains from the other enrichments of spirit, heart and body only thus to be obtained by the enlightened use of the offices of sex in the service of true love.

Harden not your hearts and say that St. Paul and his followers gave highest honours to those who were unmarried, and who were, therefore, not part of this complex unit of entwined dissimilar powers; for the words of St. Paul applied to his own century, to countries in which was rife the pagan debasement of the sacred rites of sex, and in which a small band of specialised and consecrated people lived to maintain the tradition of the truths given by Christ to a world as yet unready for them. To-day not a small band but the world-wide multitudes of Christian peoples ask from the Ministers of God's Church His instructions concerning the nearest problems of their daily lives. It is no longer a matter of policy and wisdom to place the, man and woman who marry lower in your estimation than those who withdraw from the completest experience of human life. The time has now come when a higher vision of the human pair is to be accepted.

Tainted in its inception by contact with pagan degeneracy, against which the Early Fathers revolted, the Church, even to this day, maintains many tenets and many indications of her debasement of the highest of God's mysteries expressed in human life. Thus is given a bent against the truest human rectitude God ordained, and thus sin has been multiplied in the world where pure beauty should have been generated by love. Thus those who married in vernal purity and whose true hearts led them into God's pastures from the hard road which the Church set were coerced to express their love hastily and furtively, and as though with shame they performed the act of union in such a way that not only was the spirit wounded but the flesh deprived of the influx of strength and the due balance and vitality which the act should confer.

The Church has long urged "self-restraint" upon its members, but in course of time there have grown up three divers meanings of this word, and to-day it covers abuses of the body which are unsuspected by many who use the phrase to describe complete denial of bodily contact between men and women. By some ascetic-minded Ministers "self-restraint" is urged in simple faith in this sense, but it may be and often is misunderstood by the laity to mean what other Ministers mean who advise their flock to use "self-restraint" so as to truncate the act of union that the vital sperm from the man does not penetrate the woman. Science shows that thus the bodies of both suffer, and with the bodies the spirits are weakened. No act of union fulfils the Law of God unless the two not only pulse together to the highest climax but also remain thereafter in a long brooding embrace without severance from each other; by which and through which only can the vital interchange be perfect, and following from which only can the love of the man toward the woman remain undiminished. For then, and then only, does the man receive back from the woman an exchange of vitality, which more than compensates for that which he has given to her. Ignorance of this truth has led the multitudes into a befouling and debasing view of the union in which the man is encouraged, even by the Ministers of the Church, to look upon his own part in this holiest of all sacraments as a mere gratification of his own lust instead of a mutual enrichment for God's service. Through this error multitudes of men have missed the compensating return from the woman, and, therefore, have felt a reaction of dullness or of active dislike against their partners, which reactions have caused untold sorrow, humiliation and weakness to women who would otherwise have been radiant and joyous reflections of God's love on earth. To this error do many fallen women owe their fall; through this error are many angry words spoken in matrimony. This error has also led many of you Ministers of the Church into the false belief that you preserve your purity and your vigour only in celibacy. This, if you are normal and not pre-destined ascetic men, is not so: though it may be better to be celibate than to befoul the marriage act through ignorance or a false code. This error, too, has led some of the Ministers of the Church to give instruction to the youths committed to their charge that they shall exercise what they falsely call "self-restraint" by means of wasting their own sacred secretions by their own hands, thus keeping themselves altogether from the love of wedlock. Such evil-doers also pander to their own conceit in hollow words claiming that they are "self-restrained," the while they perform one of the most impious acts which a grown man, free to unite himself with a woman, may commit. True self-restraint is not that which permits the body to cheat its own parts of their functions.

Science has revealed that each act of bodily union between a man and a woman is a three-fold consummation. In the days of St. Paul and the Early Fathers the triple complexity and vital uses of the union were not perceivable, and only its grosser uses or abuses were evident. But, to-day, God through Science has revealed the meaning of the triple function. In each act is set free not only the vital sperm, one of which may generate the body of a new human being, but there are also set free a rich and complex variety of the secretions from the sex glands of each body the balance and functioning of which control an immense number of the human faculties. A resolution of nervous and electrical tension also accompanies this, which is a part of the physical expression of the intense superphysical feeling of the true love of the mates united as one.

Thus, even by those who are married but who cannot bear children, the marital union to its fullest extent is an experience to be desired and repeated in due season so that each individual may gain the poise and enrichment which are the prerogative of those forming a well-balanced pair.

Further care is due from those who may be parents. Not only is there a setting free of complex secretions, both by the man and the woman, which they exchange, but a healthy and virile man implants six hundred million vital sperm cells in each act of union. Each one of these millions of minute and invisible animalculae may be potent to fertilise the corresponding cell in a woman.

Therefore the act of union in itself is not a concentrated and highly specialised contrivance for the exact fertilisation by each male sperm of a corresponding egg cell.

Science reveals that the act of union is not, as the Christian Churches have mistakenly maintained, designed solely for the purpose of generating children. It is in human beings the complex source of various blessings, still far from specialised and adapted. Indeed were it of use solely for procreation it would be a wasteful and archaic remnant in us of a design planned for creatures who swarmed multitudinously in the waters of the deep sea. Yet, through its other purposes in this complex act, we see mingled with this still unspecialised and scarce adjusted mechanism the basis of the mutual exchanges of man and woman, which are higher in their complexity and potentiality for good than anything conceived in the structure of any other creature. It is due to these other aspects of their union that mankind may be so far above our fellows the other animals as to be but a little lower than the angels.

Some there are among you who have maintained and would lead the people to believe that we human beings should look upon our mating unions as being solely for the purpose of the procreation of young, and we should consummate this union only once in each yearly season, as do the larger wild creatures. But this is a blindness and confusion of thought due to the formation of opinion before the revelations of Science were permitted by God.

Yet, with all the super-added and profounder significance of the functions of sex in man, there remains, in each completed union, the setting free of millions of active sperms any one of which may initiate procreation. And if man will use his highest function in the highest way he must with wisdom and knowledge so control this most archaic of his vestigial functions that injury and weakness shall not ensue to the mother and the child by too hasty crowding of young within her womb, but that, to the glory of God, immortal souls may be incarnate only in due times and seasons and well caparisoned by love.

In the procreation of children a man and a woman unite with God in the work of creation, creating not a lower and material world, but that highest of God's mundane works a human body as the habitation of a soul.

For those who would use for the service of God and man these profounder reactions of the complex union and who are already duly parents, or who for racial reasons dare not take upon them the charge of parenthood, there are problems, hitherto dark, but now illuminated.

Through all the centuries until the present time Ministers of the Churches, perceiving the wonder of life in parental creation and still uninstructed by direct revelation, have commanded that no control shall be exercised over the procreation of children.

But harden not your hearts to the new revelation and the new instruction. God through Science has revealed the powers and the value of the sacred act. God through Science has revealed the archaic output of multitudinous potential fertilisations inherently doomed. God through Science shows that the triple consummation of the marital rite shall be controlled by the uniting pair so that the enrichment of the union shall be partaken of, and, at the same time, a human life shall be brought into the world only under due conditions of pre-arranged love and forethought. To exert the righteous control of conception by the best means placed at man's service by Science is a command of God.

Concerning the control of conception, the Bishops of the Anglican Church pronounced a verdict more than a decade ago. Therein they recognised that children should not be hurled unthinkingly upon the world, and advised that parents are justified in making some effort to control their number. Nevertheless, while the Bishops condemned the application of all scientific knowledge, they permitted the limiting of the act of union to that portion of each lunar month which, in a woman, is supposed to be "safe" from the power to conceive. In this, once again, as she still lacked God's clear revelation, the Church became a blind leader of the blind and the cause of various complex sins. The instructions given by the Anglican Bishops incite man and woman to defy the law of God and Nature clearly expressed in the complete and unwarped woman's physiological rhythm, and to deprive her of union when it is physiologically best for her, while this advice allows union when it is physiologically worst: in this way, moreover, they make into an affair of unnatural times and seasons what should be a beautiful, gracious, and nature-inspired act. Furthermore, on the part of the Bishops and the clergy who give such advice an error is committed, for they mislead multitudes to a false sense of security, or, even, they lead them to hypocrisy and pretence. Woe unto him who places a stumbling-block in the path of these little ones!

Exact observation shows that there are three great varieties of mankind in our modern peoples. The type from which most often the clergy, teachers, and speakers are drawn is the ascetic type, of inactive sex vitality. These often, indeed, impoverish or upset the balance of the whole system by repression of sex expression, but, nevertheless, they can and do diminish the surface urgency of the sex functions. With narrowed understanding, perceiving not the nature of the two other and much larger classes of humanity, these endeavour to impose upon the others standards which violate their inborn nature, and give as truths statements which the inborn nature of the other types proves to be lies.

Moreover, doing this together with the worst of all faults, self-righteousness and a claim of virtue. There is in the type of woman corresponding to the ascetic man a true "safe" period, a period when physiologically she cannot be fertile, but for multitudes constructed upon another scale there is no "safe" period, and the Ministers of the Church, by recommending the use of the "safe" period as the only allowable means of controlling conception, are not only misleading these multitudes but bringing the judgment of the Church into contempt.

There are at present known to Science two or three sound physiological ways of controlling conception. In order not to thwart the other designs and purposes of the sex act, the means used to control conception must permit of the entry, the mingling and the mutual exchange of secretions between the man's uncovered organ and the woman's. God through Science shows how this may be done. At the same time, it is possible to separate the results of the act of union and obtain the vitalising mutual exchanges in every union, while from some unions only, and those selected with prayer and God's blessing, children as desired and provided for may be procreated.

In the name of God, I call upon you Ministers of the Church to listen to the revelations God makes through Science, to listen to the extension of Christ's teaching, and so to instruct your flocks that the pure and holy sacrament of marriage may no longer be debased and befouled by the archaic ignorances of centuries, and by the warping first given to the views of sex under conditions and periods utterly different from those now existing.

Harden not your hearts, O leaders of the Christian Churches. Desire no longer to maintain in bondage the rich new spirit of life springing upwards ever higher and higher in the service of God. Rise to meet the new revelation. Perceive and bow the knee to the mystery of the sanctity of marriage, the complex powers of good in the truly welded pair, the holiness and divine beauty of the union of loving and lifelong mates. Perceive that in our midst the highest expression of human life is the pair united in profound and complex union, who use the means which God now sends through Science to raise the race. These shall lead the peoples of all the world to a higher potentiality for His service than ever has been known.

Moses, learned in the wisdom of all the Egyptians, led the people into the promised land and gave them new laws. Since then humanity has travelled far upon its way Godward. To-day, learned in the revelations of Science and of God through Nature, the leader must be followed by the hearts and understandings of the people, whose feet still tread upon the soil of the land they now inhabit and whose hearts obey the new laws given in these times present. In this Gospel is written part of God's latest Revelation.

The Control of Parenthood: Imperial and Racial Aspects

From *The Control of Parenthood* (1920)

Edited by James Marchant

London: G. P. Putnam's Sons

THE vision of what the human race may one day become has hovered for many centuries over the minds of the greater thinkers and teachers. Utopias have been written picturing our wonderful development in the distant future, when humanity shall be dwelling in perfect harmony with ideal surroundings. An extension of the powers of human beings, an increase in their beauty or in the intricate workings of their minds are postulated deliberately or are implied by all the writers of Utopias; but the dreams of the Utopians of every type hovered and still hover unattached to the solid earth on which we walk; the connecting link between the present and these airy futures is never forged and placed at the disposal of humanity by the creators of visions splendid.

The race needs to be led into the promised land, and the path clearly marked which will lead directly from the grey present to the future glorious state. To-day the multitudes are too great to be led literally and physically into some new and narrow region of the earth. It is within the lands in which they now dwell that the people must be transformed and led into greater perfection of physical, mental, and spiritual beauty.

If, then, we are to find the way into Utopia while still remaining on the soil we now tread, it is *in* ourselves that we must work the transformation. Is that possible? Not as individuals but as a race it appears to me to be not only possible but within our reach. Those who are grown up in the present active generations, the matured and hardened, with all their weaknesses and flaws, cannot do very much, though they may do something, with themselves. They can, however, study the conditions under which they came into being, discover where lie the chief sources of defect, and eliminate those sources of defect from the coming generation, so as to remove from those who are still to be born the needless burdens the race has carried.

The first step into the new Utopia is the reverent and honest realisation of the miraculous power of understanding love coupled with a humble recognition of the great essential fact that human individuals are biological units in their bodily sense, just as are individual animals, plants or trees. Throughout the animal world, and throughout even the plant world there has been a continuous trend of reduction in the *number* of offspring, and an increase in the security and endowment of the offspring produced. Yet even to-day the universal law of all reproductive life is to produce innumerably more offspring than can possibly survive. Each young struggling life once endowed with an embryonic body has an amazing vitality and zest for living, and the result of this is that each will cling to life wherever it is possible to retain a foothold. Yet where they are crowded, each individual is robbing its neighbour of necessary light, space, and food, dwarfing and stunting each and all. A very simple illustration of this law can be demonstrated by planting on two plots of the same ground each six feet square, in one, two dozen and in the other two hundred plants of the same sort (for instance Shirley poppies), and allowing them to grow to maturity. In the first plot those that have room spread their leaves to the sun and air and grow to handsome individuals, in the second the spindly, small, undeveloped stems support leaves which are fighting for the light and air, and if the plants bloom at all they do so with undersized flowers. In the former the blossoms are three or four inches in diameter; in the latter the shabby flowers may be half an inch or less across. Yet even the starved and stunted flowers will go on producing their like, crowding each other to death, until probably, in the course of nature, that plot of ground is captured by a few isolated seedlings of some totally different type which, coming in small numbers, each develop sturdily, taking all the space.

Humanity is now beginning to awaken to the puny and degenerate condition of innumerable thousands, particularly in the cities, where an observant eye may often search long for a fine healthy-looking individual.

The sad features of racial degeneration which assail us on every side to-day are nearly all the result of two great wrongs. One is *crowding,* and the other the devastating infections known as Venereal Diseases.

The elimination of sex disease, because of its more rapidly contagious nature, is in some respects the most urgent problem immediately facing humanity, and were we brave enough to take this appalling scourge in the open and fight it with every sort of knowledge that is available, its evils might be rapidly curbed. So terrible are the results, particularly of syphilis, upon the next generation, that all who think agree that no diseased person should risk the transmission of such curses to his offspring. In whatever form the diseased person may protect the next generation, whether by refraining from marriage, or by separation from his wife within marriage, this is *in principle* a form of control of conception, a form which all the Churches and all thinking people must insist is the barest racial necessity.

So acute have recent events made these problems of the sex and other heritable diseases, that there is little doubt that humanity will be driven to deal frankly with the problem and to eliminate such contagions, as they have well-nigh eliminated small-pox and leprosy from this country.

In a sense disease may be looked upon as an abnormality, an unnatural and repulsive condition which a normal healthy mind revolts from and conquers, and it is therefore less dangerous to the race in some ways than a deleterious condition considered 'natural.'

The former of the two great sources of the weakening of the human stock, namely crowding, is the more fundamental, because an ever-present source of weakness, even in healthy stocks of normal, happy, untainted people. Hence crowding is, in my opinion, even more serious a menace to humanity than an open enemy like disease.

Crowding before birth, crowding in the womb of the overburdened mother, is at present the greatest of all natural sources of the dwarfing and stunting of humanity, sapping the resources of the race in every direction. And this will forever remain until humanity takes complete control of its conceptions. Sex disease may—should—be speedily eliminated, but the impulse to overpopulate is an inherent characteristic in untutored humanity. Little is realised by the general public of the immensity of the effects of this crowding in the womb of the ignorant and helpless woman, of the torment she endures, of the weakening of the human stock which results. Too little has it been realised that it is this antenatal as well as post-natal crowding that has been warping the race, so that I must make this more apparent.

Early and late Nature provides a possibility for the establishment of the human embryo in the soil of its mother's body. Crowding through her into the world comes a perpetual stream of potential lives. If each is to develop to anything like its potential perfection, it must be given space and time to grow, just as the poppy seed must have space to grow in the soil. When one embryo has established itself it can hold at bay the others for the nine months, taking all for itself, and developing by using the strength of its mother. But, directly it is separated from her, the onrush of the other potential individuals begins again, and if then another and another repeatedly takes root, each does so in a physical substratum successively weakened by what it has given to its immediate predecessor. Yet still the resources of vitality are great, and in repeated and immediate succession two, three, four, or perhaps more fresh lives may, without too great disaster, grow closely adjacent in time, if the original mother-stock is strong. But, as in the plot overplanted with the poppy seedlings, crowding, once it has reached the point of intensity, will begin to show in the punier size and weakening of the human individuals. *We are accustomed to think of crowds as being coincident in space and time, but I should like the thought to penetrate our social consciousness that in the womb the time factor which makes the crowd may be extended.*

These are physical facts. There are other and subtler results from crowding. The race pictured in the Utopias—the human race as it may be—must have not only well-developed and sufficiently beautiful and adaptable bodies, it must have minds increasingly attuned to the ideal. The effect of its environment on the mind has been partly veiled by the marvelous mastery which at times the mind may show over its physical environment. But a deep underlying truth is the fact that the expression of the potentialities of a mind depend on the bodily form through which they act, as does the electric current depend on the wires of the lamp for its transmutation into light.

What of the minds that are formed in the crowded spaces of an overburdened mother? Can they be well formed in the poison of bitterness provoked by the anguish and horror of undesired maternity? Sometimes, by rare chance, it may *appear* that this is so, although unless the whole life in its most secret and inmost recesses is laid bare, who is to say how much any individual may to-day suffer secretly and in bravely hidden mental depression as a result of the secret misery of his mother while she carried him?

The credulous reliance which humanity is encouraged to place on any pronouncement supposedly of 'science,' when uttered authoritatively, has often led humanity astray, or at least by a very zigzag and convoluted path in the direction of the real truth. Not the least of the injuries done to the human race by the partial misapprehension of greater truths has been the 'scientific' derision of the view that the mother's mental state affects the child during the nine months she carries it before birth. A few of the prophets of science, wiser than the majority, have recognised the possibility of antenatal influence, as did Alfred Russell Wallace; but modern science is only just beginning to discover the necessary analogous facts which will some day make clear and demonstrate this truth. In my opinion the truth of ante-natal influence through the mother is certain, so that not only the bodily condition, but the mental and spiritual outlook, of the mother affects the child she is bearing. For the purpose of this essay I take the above view as axiomatic, for there is not space here to discuss the evidence.

What can be the effect of the working of this law on the race? Do we not see it all round us in the bitterness, the hatred, the inhuman virulence of one human being towards another? Such dispositions are the very counterpart of the feelings of outraged horror and revolt which overwhelm the already overburdened mother, when she feels the drag within her of yet another child she did not desire.

It is sometimes carelessly argued that all through the centuries of the past women have always been involuntary mothers, and that the human race in times past had a greater physical perfection than it has to-day. Our knowledge of the past is partial, a few mountain peaks lit by sunlight stand out of the crowded and hazy glimpses of the forgotten, and we see figures of the stalwart Viking, the beautiful Greek, the proud Egyptian. The misty uncertainty of our knowledge of ancient times covers the myriads who have crowded into life merely to be extinguished or suppressed by early death. Look at the tombs of the fifteenth and sixteenth centuries in our churches, where the rows of sons and daughters carved upon the sides of the tombs are so frequently infants and young children who have died within a year or two of birth! It is true that in those days, in all the days until quite recent times, most women have borne meekly and unresistingly the burden of crowded lives, borne them perhaps without any voiced—perhaps without any conscious—feeling of revolt. The revolt, the bitterness, which is now finding expression in violence and uprising in every quarter of the world, is the result not only of simple crowding, but is also the echo of the revolt and bitterness and horror of women who bore that burden of age-long tradition, no longer passively, but *bearing it with the consciousness that it should not have been* if they had been allowed full knowledge.

For nearly one hundred years there has been in the world knowledge which might long ago have been universal property, which could have prevented every dreaded conception, which could have saved anguish and burden and deformity colossal in its harrowing amount. This knowledge has been withheld from womanhood nearly all over the world, but it has not been annihilated. Echoes of its existence, of its beneficent potentialities have traveled from one to the other. The most overburdened, the most ignorant, has faintly and vaguely realised that things need not be so cruel for her as they are. The human mind, tormented in any way, bows itself and can almost forget the anguish if it is a fundamental necessity (as humanity, tormented by the shortness of life and the imminence of death, forgets these things and laughs and dances), yet it will not so patiently endure torment, burdens, wrongs which it consciously realises are not fundamental necessities, which are indeed *imposed* upon it by others, collectively or individually.

For more than a generation women throughout the world, sometimes clearly, sometimes with but a glimmering, have realised that the age-long burden and outrage of the overcrowded womb is not a fundamental necessity. Those then who have borne more and ever more children than they desired, under conditions that outraged them, have bred into the plastic minds that were forming within them that sense of bitterness and revolt which is now so poisoning human relations.

How different the racial value of desired and beloved children! Minds surrounded by every form of healthy and beautiful mental and bodily activity are able to grow in helpful harmony. If the joyous picture of a radiantly beautiful humanity in a true Utopia is ever to be achieved, it must be achieved by creating only minds and bodies desired and beloved from the first moment of their inception.

Translated into terms of everyday practice, I maintain that the only hope for the race is the conscious elimination of all diseased and overcrowded lives *before* their conception, by planning only to conceive those for whom adequate pro-vision of material necessities and a loving welcome are reasonably to be anticipated.

When once the women of *all* classes have the fear and dread of undesired maternity removed from them, they will be free to put all their delicate strength into creating desired and beautiful children. And it is on the feet of those children that the race will go forward into the promised land of Utopia.

This, the first foundation of Utopia, could be reached in my lifetime, had I the power to issue inviolable edicts. Alas I, that the age of a beneficent autocracy has never been and is not here to-day! Instead of achieving in two generations the great result on the human race that could be materialised, it will be necessary to take the slower means of creating in every individual that intense consciousness of the race which will make it impossible for individuals ever to tolerate the coercion of enforced and miserable motherhood, with its consequent poison of the racial stream.

How Mrs. Jones Does Her Worst

London Daily Mail, June 13, 1919

OWING to the silly lies most of us were told in childhood we are afraid to face frankly the problems of birth. So as a nation we go muddling along in the way of our grandparents, and babies "come" apparently at the instigation of an ironic fairy, who brings them most frequently to women who have already had more than they want . . .

If you go down the mean streets of our cities, searching each face for its story, for its revelation of the bodily condition of its owner, and you can come back without curses on your lips for the folly and horror of the system that makes them, you are built of cast iron. Are these puny-faced, gaunt, blotchy, ill-balanced, feeble, ungainly, withered children the young of an Imperial race?

Let us stop and speak to Mrs. Jones. Ask her why she had Jennie while Tom was still less than a year old, when she had only just buried Sally on her second birthday— ask her if she thought she could do justice to children coming in rapid succession like that! If she is not dazed into stupidity by physical exhaustion she will tell you: "I knew I was too weak— but there, what is one to do? They come, bless 'em, and once the baby is there love for it seems to grow, however much you didn't want the last one!"

Jennie is white and puling, a wailing scrap. You ask her mother if she nursed Tom while Jennie was coming. "Of course I had to, with milk the price it was; I don't hold with bottle babies and doctor didn't either. My neighbour has had to use a bottle at times, poor thing, for she has had 11 children and buried 9— 11 births that is; of course, there were others that didn't get so far."

You ask her why she and her neighbour do not take control of their own and their children's health by refusing to have babies one on top of each other so that each one saps the strength of the next one and all sap the mother's strength beyond repair? She will answer: "What can a poor woman do?"

Now is it for Mrs. Jones to take the initiative? Isn't it for the leisured, the wise, to go to her and tell her what are the facts of life, the meaning of what she is doing, and what she ought to do?

The serious truth is that not many of the leisured and learned have bothered to think out the meaning of what she is doing. If they realized it, surely an outcry of dismay would be raised, *for Mrs. Jones is destroying the race!*

Strong, healthy men and women— men "fit" enough for the Army, even if they are at work in times of peace; women strong enough to be glad mates to men are needed by the State in ever-increasing numbers.

What is Mrs. Jones providing for the State, at great cost, and at perpetually recurrent agony to herself? Nine times in twelve years she produced a potential citizen. Of these, six died were expensively buried before they were two years old; one lived who somehow was not "all there"; two others live, but one of these has bad teeth and the other, as Mrs. Jones herself said, "was never strong. How could you expect it when he came so soon after the sixth— ten and a half months it was, and he so small I never thought to rear him!"

From Mrs. Jones's family, then, the State receives two workers, neither "fit" enough for the Army, and it has the debit account of a feeble-minded child, later to be a burden as a potential pauper. The State loses nine times over the healthy work of Mrs. Jones for varying periods, it loses the labour spent on babies' coffins, and it loses the vitality and joy which a healthy Mrs. Jones might have radiated. The cost to Mrs. Jones herself— only a woman can guess.

Now, is that account between Mrs. Jones and the State *business?* I am saying nothing about the sentiment of it. Let Mrs. Jones only have two *healthy* children and no more, and the State would at once gain; let her have three healthy children and they would be out of all proportion more valuable to the State than the three she has.

Now, why should Mrs. Jones and the State between them suffer the ill-health, the loss, the birth agonies nine times over for two unsatisfactory results, when she might have had a reasonable expectation of producing three or four good children from three or four carefully arranged, controlled and cared for births?

Why? She needed the knowledge of what is called "birth control" to begin with. Why did she not have it? Echo answers, because of our national stupidity, prudery, and barbarism. The conditions of modern life are a defiance of "Nature," and yet we do not equip the mothers of the race with the knowledge necessary wisely to control the unnatural conditions of life in which they find themselves.

A Letter to Working Mothers (1919)

I EXPECT your first child was a great joy to you and your husband, but you went on having children so rapidly that you got very tired and worn out by the third or fourth child, or miscarriage. Also, if they came about every year, you had not time properly to nurse one before another was on the way, and you noticed that they seemed not to be so strong as you would like. You wanted a good family, but you did so want time to rest and get strong yourself between their coming, and you so wanted that every child you bore should be strong enough to live and grow up. No one told you how to give yourself a good long interval to pick up between the children; I am going to tell you how to do this so that you may bear *strong* children, and be happy bearing the children, because you have them when you are really *well,* and want them yourself. It gives you much pain and sorrow and loss to bear many weak children which die early, and it is also a terrible waste all round. What you would like, and what the country needs, are strong happy children who live and grow up to be fine men and women.

Also, many of those to whom I am writing this letter in particular are mothers who have already several children, and whose husbands, for one reason or another, are not able to earn very big wages; or, even worse, have gone in for drink, or who have become ill. You have a hard struggle to keep your children, and when the weekly wage is spent on rent and food, there is very little, perhaps nothing, left for many other things you need. But you are still young, and you are living with your husband, and there is always the shadow of fear hiding in the corner of your bedroom that, if you let him have his way, there will be more babies, and that will stop you working and will bring another child to feed, and you feel you cannot face it. The last one you had was very 'peeky', and you cannot afford to give it enough milk.

So you begin to dread what used to be your chief joy, that is to have your husband with you. On the other hand, if you are a strong-minded woman and you rule your husband and prevent him having his way, there is another fear, however much you may hide it deep in the bottom of your heart, and that is that you will not keep him, and that some bad girl will get him, for men who are husbands need what is wrongly called the 'husband's right'.

This makes things very difficult for you, and very often it happens that you get 'caught', and you know that the baby that you feared might come has really begun. Then your mind is full of anxiety because you fear all the extra poverty and trouble, perhaps even the hunger that it will mean, and as you love children you fear also the cruelty of bringing a little child into the world without being able to feed it, and give it the clothes it needs. So you do, or you try to do, a desperate thing: you try to get rid of that baby before it has 'gone too far'. Your neighbours or some old woman you know may tell you of various dodges which they have tried, and which may get rid of the beginning of a baby, and perhaps you try one after the other; but either it may have gone too far, or in that way you may be strong, and you may find that the little unwanted baby continues to grow.

Now I want you to think what this means, and I want you never again to try to get rid of a baby if it has begun. Many, many times the things women have done to themselves to try to get rid of a coming baby have made both themselves and that baby weaker than it would have been, perhaps even have deformed it. But babies that are coming are wonderfully strong little creatures, and possibly you may appear to have done very little harm to it; but though the harm may not show for a long time,

it is there, because you have harmed yourself, and the coming baby gets everything through you. Anything which weakens you or strains you, injures you and through you affects your child in some way, even though it may not show at first . . .

Enduring Passion
(1928)

Author's Preface (Excerpts)

I AM convinced that the more *happy*, child-bearing and *enduringly* passionate marriages there are in a State, the more firmly established is that State.

This book I offer to individuals with my love and sympathy, and in the hope that it may add to their lasting happiness: to the State I offer it because, if it should raise the standard of married happiness, it will be a greater national bulwark than many battleships.

M. C. S.

CHAPTER I

A Common Sadness

"Marriage requires to be transformed, because everything around it is transformed."—FINOT

EVERY true lover desires that love shall endure. In young lovers, the conviction flowers easily and spontaneously that their new passion is not only unique in its individual beauty, but is eternal, more lasting than life itself. Yes, even to-day, although the young achieve their mating under increasing difficulties, owing to the ever-growing vastness of cities and the individual peculiarities of civilized people, nevertheless the majority of young people love spontaneously and naturally, and hope with the eternal hope of youth.

It has been brought to my notice over and over again that an uneasiness lurks in the recesses of the minds of even the most romantic and instructed married lovers. They fear the existence of some *natural* law predestined in the end to work against them and destroy their mutual attraction. They wonder whether all the help afforded by knowledge such as I give in *Married Love* merely, at the best, secures a few years of happiness, and whether time will give that cruel law its inevitable innings and they will grow apart.

That so many pairs of happy lovers should have turned into drably tolerant married couples, or should learn positively to detest, or even to fear each other as the years pass, saddens us all.

One cannot take up a newspaper nowadays without finding articles, stories or letters, written on the assumption that, after the passing of some years, nearly every marriage will become dreary or worse. All this has a hypnotic effect on people who cannot altogether avoid the influences of "crowd sentiment." One feels that it could not take root and persist if there were not some basis of fact, or at any rate supposed fact, giving it substance. There must be something more fundamental than the accidents of time and ailments to overturn deeply rooted love, for one sees how negligible such externals may be when passion endures.

A generally felt anticipation seems to be:— That the very basis of marriage is thus attacked by the "inevitable" failure to persist, of the mutual sex attraction. That it gradually fades out altogether as does a child's sand-castle on the shore, eaten away little by little by the advancing tide of indifference, the waves of which lap forward after each act of union in the trough of despondency or indifference which follows it.

It is widely assumed that in the path of those who have been married for some time stalks the apparently unconquerable dragon, the doom of all mating humanity for centuries, whose form and ramifications are hinted at in the Latin proverb: "Post coitum omne triste," or "Omne animal post coitum triste." (After coitus all are depressed.)

This conception has colored innumerable creative minds; tinged with asceticism, pessimism, gloom or ribaldry the works of great masters of literature; afforded the theme of plays and poems; woven itself into the social conventions. Many a doubtful joke and story hinges upon the universal acceptance of the idea. Indeed so ingrained in human consciousness is it, so fundamentally entrenched that the vast majority of adult men really believe it. I did not deal with it, or even hint at it in *Married Love,* the book for happy youth, yet the dragon's plangency was somewhat weakened by that book. It is time it was slain by serious people and its suggestive power for evil shattered.

The chapters of this new book may at first sight appear unrelated, yet I trust they will all do their share of dragon-slaughter.

To expand the terseness of the Latin phrase so as fully to express explicitly all that it subtly implies would require many pages. As was once said to me briefly by a married man, it is that: "All the world knows after the sex act, the man is weakened and disgusted and turns away from woman for a time until his natural lust returns."

In other words it is the idea, which the experience of many people would appear to confirm, that, after the marriage act (the union of the man and the woman), the eagerness and the vitality of the man are reduced: he has used up some of his energy, and he has to recuperate thereafter. This implies that the act of union, although it may have been consummated as a result of an intense urge, and is a natural physiological demand of his body, necessitates an expenditure rather than a gaining of energy on the part of the man, and has left him with his forces temporarily reduced.

Few have combated this assumption. It is true that in his monumental work *Studies in the Psychology of Sex,* Dr. Havelock Ellis does not subscribe to this "popular fallacy," but devotes half a page to emphasize his view that "under reasonably happy circumstances there is no pain, or exhaustion, or sadness, or emotional revulsion. The happy lover's attitude toward his partner is not expressed by the well-known sonnet (cxxix) of Shakespeare:—

> 'Past reason hunted, and no sooner had
> Past reason hated.'

He feels rather with Boccaccio that the kissed mouth loses not its charm,

> 'Bocca bacilata non perde ventura.'"

How to secure and maintain the "reasonably happy circumstances" he does not tell a world deeply hungering for the information. I propose to attempt to give it such help. That it desperately needs new light on the problem of permanence of sex love in marriage leaps at one's heart.

Few men are quite as frank as was Lord X. Before I wrote this book, when in the privacy of a *tête-à-tête* in his own house, he turned upon me with bitterness for having told womanhood in my book *Married Love* of the physical joys of marriage. "What have you done?" he exclaimed. "You have broken up the home; you have let women know about things which only prostitutes ought to know; once you give women a taste for these things, they become vampires, and you have let loose vampires into decent men's homes. When we men want that sort of thing— a woman who knows how to enjoy herself in sex life— we, go to prostitutes at our own times when we feel like it. We do not want that sort of thing in our own homes. The wife should be the housekeeper and make the home a place of calm comfort for a man. Instead of that you have made my home a hell: I cannot meet the demands of my wife now she knows. If you create these vampire women, you will rear a race of effeminate men." Continuing with fury, did not this man, assailing true love, scourging me as its exponent, really reveal his own debased ideas of woman captive and enslaved in a home? For him woman should be deprived not only of the enjoyment of true sex union, but of its health-giving balance, its vitalizing power, and the very joyous sense of equality with her mate.

Woman, according to him, is to be the housekeeper, the breeder, but never his mate, his joyous companion. Selfishly he goes to the prostitute whom he can pay at his own time to simulate passion and play with him in any filthy manner that his debased taste craves.

This man is elderly. I suppose he would be in enthusiastic agreement with Acton, the classic "authority," who once said: "Happily for society the majority of women are not very much troubled with sex feelings of any kind."

The concomitant of this is evident. The sacramental and mutual character of true union is overlooked. Naturally where lust and not true love urge the pair together, after that brief union the man experiences a lack of interest, shading in some into a repulsion. In others there may even be a positive fear of the partner in union owing to the feeling that the woman has robbed them of something. Such unions do rob both man and woman of the very best and highest aspects of sex life.

One could easily fill many books if one began to elaborate and reproduce in its manifold forms and presentation throughout the romantic and scientific literature, medical treatises, common talk of country folk, and the ribald jests of the slums and the music-hall, the idea behind "Post coitum omne triste."

And now I challenge it!

I challenge, not that it is generally considered to be a fact: that is obvious! I challenge the very existence of the fact itself. I deny that it is a fact in a scientific sense. It is a phenomenon based on ignorance and folly and the hypnotism of custom. It is *not* an inherent physiological and inevitable result of the unions of an enlightened and instructed race of lovers.

I challenge the ages and the men of all ages! I tell them that this false "fact" of theirs has warped, colored and injured their lives, weakened their powers, cut at the roots of their love, eaten like a canker into their respect for womanhood, blasted and desolated homes. It is not a true fact when viewed by science. It is a chimera bred by ignorance, haunting the cloudy miasmic swamps of tradition.

Confusion and misapprehension have arisen from the hasty misunderstanding of countless men and women. Having themselves flouted Nature by thwarting her intentions; injured Nature by bending her to their will; acting wrongly because they were misinformed, they plunged themselves, and involved almost the entire human race in an intricate web of grievances and distresses— needlessly.

Some couples happily escape what is generally considered the common fate of mated mankind. Theirs are the lifelong happy marriages. They are few. One can scarcely take up the day's journal at any time without some reference to the rarity of happiness in marriage lasting over many years. When the lambent exceptions are commented upon, the suggestion is that there had been some chance combination of qualities in this man and woman, specially favored by the gods of fate, so that they have loved lastingly If questioned, the pair will generally attribute their success in marriage to some extraneous circumstances, or simply claim that they loved and knew how to love; giving so little explanatory addition that the enquiring multitude is left as uninstructed as before. The existence of such couples is a fortunate chance. It is one of the objects of this book vastly to increase the number of such couples, and not only to challenge the desolating "Post coitum omne triste," but to show in detail how it is wrong, and how that wrong may be righted.

There is nothing in the world which the human heart so desires as a steady home life, lasting and, enduring love, and the radiance of inner unity and mutual delight. No excuse is needed for attempting to contribute something which should help multitudes to secure these treasures. Who can doubt that the stability of the nation depends on the health and *happiness* of its homes? While we are human beings inhabiting this world, surely even the most presumptuous of us cannot claim to be anything higher than human. The success of our experience in life depends on an intricately interwoven but nicely balanced adjustment and satisfaction of the needs and requirements of all three factors— body, mind and spirit.

Throughout this book, I shall not attempt to disentangle these factors and to deal first in one chapter with one, and then in another with the other, for their actions and reactions are all interwoven. If I appear to emphasize the body, it is because it can be directly reached by material aids and thus assisted to be a more perfect instrument of the soul. In all chapters I will try to clarify what seem to me the salient points in the aspect of sex love therein considered. Just as when writing *Married Love* it was essential to set out the anatomical and physiological details of the sex organs, and simply to state the direct facts of coitus : so, to consider the present theme it will be essential to deal with further material facts about, and the conduct of, the act of coitus. Coitus is the kernel of physical marriage. The minutiae of the way in which sex union between man and woman is conducted give rise to other reactions, branching into many ramifications of human thought and effort.

In *Married Love* I explained why I demanded the *wooing* of the wife and the attainment of the orgasm for her as well as for her husband. The recognition, now almost universal, that this— ten years ago so audacious a demand—

is woman's legitimate right is a great step forward. But now I demand something more, another step forward in marital conduct. This time the benefit is more directly a gain to the man than to the woman, but, as in all things concerning the mutual partnership of marriage, the gain for one is the enrichment of both.

In my opinion, to establish an enduring passion in a lasting marriage it is necessary to uproot various physical faults commonly practiced which lie behind the Latin phrase "Post coitum omne triste."

CHAPTER III

Excessive "Virility" (excerpts)

The contrary case [to excessive virility], that of a woman making sex demands greater than can be met by her husband, is a creature almost unthought of by the Victorian social code. She is, however, a very real person, known to antiquity, feared throughout the ages, and perhaps now at last, as a result of the recent frank attitude towards sex and its problems, openly recognized once more. The truer statement of woman's side of the sex partnership which has characterized the last decade since *Married Love* was published, has made possible now a consideration of her problems.

I remember some years ago a Japanese professor of biology telling me that there was a proverb in his language about sex union to the effect that "As the years of marriage pass, the woman wants more and more and the man is less able to give what he has taught her to demand." This, of course, is by no means a universal position, but . . . there are a number, probably about thirty percent, of the professional and upper class married women suffering in their marriages from an insufficient virility in their husbands to meet their own physiological needs. If there is absolute impotence on the part of the man, the grievance of the woman is recognized both by Law and Church.

But the girl, once made a wife, may thereafter have so scant a fare of the feasts of love as, literally, to be starved. What of a woman whose sex needs are such that she is left either below par and dissatisfied or really physically unhappy, almost ill, without frequent sex union, if her husband, while being not abnormally undersexed, yet is unable to meet her demands? Many women suffer frightfully in secret when placed in such a position in a "civilized" community. I am inclined to think that a large number of those in a "neurotic" condition, sufferers from sleeplessness, bad temper, indigestion and so on, are the victims of sex-deprivation. The profounder needs of their whole organisms are not being met.

Can anything be done? Of course *self* stimulus, or masturbation, is extremely common. It is used by married women whose husbands, having stimulated them, leave them in "mid-air" with no orgasm, causing nervous irritation. Masturbation is *not* the proper remedy, and a careful husband should secure orgasm for his wife. Masturbation is *always* unsatisfactory for various reasons, including those mentioned on this page. Another practical solution which some deprived women find is in Lesbian love with their own sex. The other, and quite correct name for what is now so often euphemistically called Lesbian love is homosexual vice. It is so much practiced nowadays, particularly by the "independent" type of woman, that I run a risk of being attacked because I call the thing by its correct name. One of the physical results of such unnatural relations is the gradual accustoming of the system to reactions which are arrived at by a different process from that for which the parts were naturally formed. This tends to unfit women for real union. If a married woman does this unnatural thing she may find a growing disappointment in her husband and he may lose all natural power to play his proper part. . . No woman who values the peace of her home and the love of her husband should yield to the wiles of the Lesbian whatever the temptation to do so may be.

A very *very* few women have strong inborn tendencies of this type; most of those now indulging in the vice drifted into it lazily or out of curiosity and allowed themselves to be corrupted. This corruption spreads as an underground fire spreads in the peaty soil of a dry moorland. Men with an excess of the "feminine" qualities and "masculine" women are, by the inherent bias given to their emotions by their physical equipment, very liable to enter into some degree or other of the many possible relationships with their own accredited sex. They may marry and yet have disastrous homosexual entanglements. Phases of the problems raised by such people seem to me to call for recognition, yet they lead us away from the theme of this book into difficult realms. I do not want to discuss homosexuality. Nevertheless I do want people to understand what seems to me a vital scientific argument against it untinged with any of the simple, old-fashioned objections now so often repudiated. The bedrock objection to it is surely that women can only play with each other and *cannot* in the very nature of things have natural union or supply each other with the seminal and prostatic secretions which they ought to have, and crave for unconsciously.

Hence, homosexual excitement does not really meet their need, for the physiological fact (I have never yet seen it clearly stated anywhere, but it is of the greatest importance in a consideration of this problem) that, apart from the kisses, endearment, flattery, and love-making from her husband, a woman's need and *hunger* nourishment in sex union is a true union is a true physiological hunger to be satisfied only by the supplying of the actual molecular substances lacked by her system. Lesbian love, as the alternative, is NOT a real equivalent and merely soothes perhaps and satisfies no more than the surface nervous excitement. It does not, and by its nature it can never supply the actual physiological nourishment, the chemical molecules produced by the accessory glandular systems of the male. These are supplied to the woman's system when the normal act of union is experienced, and the man's secretions are deposited in her body together with the semen.

Dr. Maxwell Telling says about this: "I am not so near conviction about this as you appear to be, though I should like to be. To physiologists the true function of the prostatic fluid is still unknown : so far as I am aware it has not passed beyond the 'to dilate and give bulk to the semen' hypothesis of my student days. Contrasted with this your theory *is* at least attractive."

After I published *Wise Parenthood* some years ago, Sir William Arbuthnot Lane, the famous surgeon, told me of some interesting cases of his own which certainly seemed to indicate that part at least of the prostatic secretion is beneficially absorbed by the woman from the male ejaculate deposited in her vagina. This appeared to me to be of immense value in various ways, and to afford a key-explanation of a variety of phenomena. Since then I have followed up and studied the effect myself. I have come to the conclusion that there undoubtedly is a real physiological hunger for the chemical and complex molecular substances found in the accessory glands of the male, which can be supplied to women who unconsciously feel their need and show it in the apparently irrelevant but really quite direct way of inviting sex union in what appears excessive amounts from their mates. Or, sometimes, from lovers in addition to their husbands.

Such women are constantly sneered at or laughed at or made the butts of ignorant and vulgar jokes— but who has studied and helped them? Just a few medical men have "cured" a few of them as private patients by giving them certain glandular extracts. I know of no fair and kindly and open consideration of their needs. I think a frank and fundamental statement of the facts will do something to alter public opinion and clean up the foetid atmosphere round the whole subject.

It has been found possible to prepare some at least of the very molecular compounds really nourishing to the woman's system, and which she lacks and requires. These may be prepared so as to preserve their chemical qualities, and presented in such a way that they can be swallowed by the mouth in ordinary gelatine capsules. These capsules are just like those in which many, other medicines are prescribed and taken in order to meet a great range and variety of requirements in modern civilized people.

Some medical practitioners administer such glandular extracts by direct *injection* instead of by the mouth, but I do not at all advise injection for a great variety of reasons which would take one too far to discuss. But one simple reason may be readily grasped: We cannot by any human process exactly simulate the way these glandular extracts naturally enter the blood and lymph streams by infinitesimal amounts *continuously*. The best we can do is to take several small doses a day, and to do this we can, without too great a strain on the memory, manage, say, to swallow a capsule three times daily, and carry this on for several months. But can one possibly ask or expect a busy medical practitioner to give his time and attention to administer three injections a day for months to an individual who is approximately well anyway, and only requires better "balance" and "toning up"?

Moreover, who (even if the time could be spared) would choose to be injected three times a day for months if it could be avoided? No healthy minded person.

Some practitioners formerly having tried makes of extracts for use by the mouth which proved unsatisfactory, distrust all such. But there are now available reliable ones, and without doubt their manufacture will rapidly improve till all and not only a few firms can supply satisfactory substances. I cannot refrain from urging all my readers to avoid every possible puncture of the skin. *Never* be injected with anything if it is possible to avoid it. There may be times in acute and specific *disease* or threatened disease when injection is not to be avoided, but I am not now discussing *disease* at all.

In view of much vague and hysterical talk on the subject of "glands" and especially "monkey glands", I want to make it clear that I am not proposing the use of monkey glands at all and do not in any circumstances recommend them.

I should like my readers to realize how, by our unnatural ideas about eating, we deprive our systems of many parts of the animals which help to keep wild animals healthy, just as we lose all sorts of valuable mineral salts by throwing away the water in which we have been boiling vegetables. Then our systems may find a lack of, say, phosphorus compounds or iron compounds. When we lack these minerals we at once (if we are wise) reform our way of life, and meanwhile to restore ourselves swallow some mineral compounds in the form of "medicine" to supply to our alimentary canals the compounds from which our system is suffering a shortage; these are transmitted to the blood or lymph streams and thus supplied to the various tissues requiring these chemical molecules. Our cells then, successfully, carry on their work again. Now it has recently been discovered that by careful laboratory technique certain more complex chemical molecules given out by the various glands, can be isolated and "extracted" and specially prepared so that they too can be swallowed as "medicine." When it becomes evident that one or more of these types of chemical compounds is lacking they can be swallowed, enter the alimentary canal, and thence are transmitted to the blood or lymph streams and thus supplied to the various tissues requiring these chemical molecules. Our cells then, successfully, carry on their work again. The compounds are quite harmless and are effective.

Quite apart from the emotional loss in the absence of romance and sentiment, the sex-starved woman, in my opinion, is one whose system is not supplied with the necessary amount of certain complex chemical molecules produced in the prostatic glands. If then she will swallow the properly prepared extracts of these glands in suitable quantities for her own requirements, she should, by nourishing her system properly as it demands, not only enhance its general physiological condition, but mitigate the distressing *social* symptoms involved.

For some sex-starved women the prostatic extract alone is very effective, sometimes prostatic and orchic extract should be mixed. For others, those for instance with a markedly "run down" condition, the addition of chemical compounds of glycero-phosphates of calcium and other elements is useful.

It is very important that the extracts should be expertly and freshly made, and I trust the above clear statement of the *why* of the usefulness of such preparations will not lead women to take dry tablets and all kinds of "patent medicine" or quack nostrums which are soon sure to, if they do not already, abound on the market. Such a subject is too often surrounded by so much mystery that both the patient and the practitioner are shy of approaching or discussing it, and hence advice from commercial firms and quacks is often taken instead of proper medical advice. I do urge everyone to go only to reliable practitioners about such subjects. I feel that possibly the open and simple explanations given in this book may make it easier than it has been hitherto for people needing such help to go to their own doctors for the prescriptions. I do urge everyone *not* to take these or any prescriptions in the book without consultation with their medical attendant, and also I urge them not to increase the prescribed dose. It is such a common mistake to imagine that because one capsule or pill or teaspoonful of; anything is prescribed and seems to do good, that two or more of the same will do more good. An increased dose may often not only fail to do more good but may do active harm by upsetting the glandular balance in a fresh direction.

To take into the alimentary canal as nourishment chemical compounds of which our artificial mode of life deprives us is not only simple common sense, but is to conform to the custom we indulge in at every meal— eating what we need to carry on our fife-functioning.

The idea of *eating* to avoid fornication may appear— perhaps like all the new ideas of science it actually is— startling.

On consideration I think it will be realized by humanity not only as sound common sense, but also as a clean, wholesome, unexciting way of disposing of one of the most agonizing, torturing worries of body and spirit which has burdened the shoulders of life's struggling pilgrims till they have sweated and panted and agonized in prayer. Eat—wisely. Lo! the burden will be lightened and may even roll off, and a once tormented woman can step lightly and happily forward.

Such nourishing capsules to assuage the sex hunger in deprived women should be of great use to three types of the strongly sexed:

(1) The loving wife accustomed to sex union with her husband in marriage, who is parted from him perforce when one of them is in a far country or they are separated owing to business or perhaps by the illness of one of the married pair.

(2) Then, too, there are women, whose husbands may be with them, and may be doing their "duty" (as it is sometimes rather crudely called), yet who find that insufficient to meet the needs of the personal equation. They may with advantage supplement the amounts of glandular secretion which they obtain so as to meet their specially high requirements by taking these capsules at intervals when they feel the need.

(3) Then, too, there are those who are unmarried, and who at periodic intervals feel the passionate need of sex union, and yet, having a moral sense well developed and a recognition of the present social code, hesitate to have union outside marriage, and suffer (some of them suffer excessively) at recurrent intervals. Many such women would be definitely helped by taking such capsules for two or three days at the times of such spontaneous sex excitement.

This book is for the married, so here I do, no more than point out their obvious value to strongly sexed unmarried women who desire to lead chaste lives.

I think such utilization of the advances of modern science and the employment of glandular compounds for this purpose is one of the most potentially useful and socially valuable applications of modern research.

The report of a medical practitioner may be of interest here. He used prostatic extract for "an obscure nervous condition in an unmarried woman aged 35 years." "For several years she has suffered from what was termed by a neurologist, who examined her, 'sexual neurasthenia.' She also had melancholia and tachycardia." She took prostatic gland extract for two months and "she is very much improved. Her nervous and mental symptoms have cleared up, the pulse rate has reduced from 110 to 80; she has a cheerful outlook on life and her friends remark upon the wonderful change in her."

There is no doubt at all that numbers of unbalanced, sex-starved women in a community cannot fail to be a source of friction to others, and certainly of dissatisfaction and unhappiness to themselves.

It is perfectly right and proper that priests and pastors should preach continence and self-control. I too advise the use of both these, and indeed every mental aid to a well-balanced sex life. Yet doubtless as the truth is understood, it will increasingly be recognized that where there is a definite physiological deficit, a physiological hunger for certain chemical molecules, you might as well dangle a sugar cake in front of a child starving for its dinner and tell it not to cry but to exercise self-control, as to preach self-control unaided by physiological nourishment to a human being whose sex-system cries out for chemical molecules. Science can now isolate and supply the molecules suited to that system. Would it not be cruel to withhold that knowledge from use? It is a different thing to preach self-control to a nature reasonably nourished. For the first time in history our generation finds it possible to give some practical help to those naturally so strongly sexed that "self-control" becomes almost a physical impossibility through the frantic urge of physiological starvation. They may by quietly swallowing the glandular compounds they lack, assist themselves to become devout, and less the slave of nature's demands for the enjoyment of the other sex. So much the better for mankind. Warped strivings and "kicking against the pricks" have never helped humanity forward. But a wise use of Nature's potential riches brings abundant rewards.

Made in the
USA
Middletown, DE